Alternatives and Futures: Cultures, Practices, Activism and Utopias

Series Editor
Anitra Nelson
Melbourne Sustainable Society Institute
The University of Melbourne
Melbourne, VIC, Australia

Movements such as degrowth, Occupy, solidarity economies, permaculture, low impact living and Via Campesina variously address key issues of the contemporary era such as inequalities of wealth and income, environmental crises, and achieving sustainable cities and production. This series demonstrates the breadth, depth, significance and potential of 'alternatives' in the construction of this century, focusing on the type of future each movement advocates and their strategic agenda.

Alternatives and Futures is of interest to scholars and students across the social sciences and humanities, especially those working in environmental sustainability, politics and policymaking, environmental justice, grassroots governance, heterodox economics and activism.

The series offers a forum for constructive critique and analytical reflection of movements' directions, activism and activists, their assumptions, drivers, aims, visions of alternative futures and actual performance and influence.

More information about this series at
http://www.palgrave.com/gp/series/15864

Samuel Alexander
Sangeetha Chandrashekeran
Brendan Gleeson
Editors

Post-Capitalist Futures

Paradigms, Politics, and Prospects

Editors
Samuel Alexander
Melbourne Sustainable Society Institute
University of Melbourne
Parkville, VIC, Australia

Sangeetha Chandrashekeran
Melbourne Sustainable Society Institute
University of Melbourne
Parkville, VIC, Australia

Brendan Gleeson
Melbourne Sustainable Society Institute
University of Melbourne
Parkville, VIC, Australia

ISSN 2523-7063   ISSN 2523-7071 (electronic)
Alternatives and Futures: Cultures, Practices, Activism and Utopias
ISBN 978-981-16-6529-5   ISBN 978-981-16-6530-1 (eBook)
https://doi.org/10.1007/978-981-16-6530-1

© The Editor(s) (if applicable) and The Author(s), under exclusive licence to Springer Nature Singapore Pte Ltd. 2022
This work is subject to copyright. All rights are solely and exclusively licensed by the Publisher, whether the whole or part of the material is concerned, specifically the rights of translation, reprinting, reuse of illustrations, recitation, broadcasting, reproduction on microfilms or in any other physical way, and transmission or information storage and retrieval, electronic adaptation, computer software, or by similar or dissimilar methodology now known or hereafter developed.
The use of general descriptive names, registered names, trademarks, service marks, etc. in this publication does not imply, even in the absence of a specific statement, that such names are exempt from the relevant protective laws and regulations and therefore free for general use.
The publisher, the authors and the editors are safe to assume that the advice and information in this book are believed to be true and accurate at the date of publication. Neither the publisher nor the authors or the editors give a warranty, expressed or implied, with respect to the material contained herein or for any errors or omissions that may have been made. The publisher remains neutral with regard to jurisdictional claims in published maps and institutional affiliations.

Cover Pattern © John Rawsterne/patternhead.com

This Palgrave Macmillan imprint is published by the registered company Springer Nature Singapore Pte Ltd.
The registered company address is: 152 Beach Road, #21-01/04 Gateway East, Singapore 189721, Singapore

Series Preface for *Post-Capitalist Futures*

The *Alternatives and Futures: Cultures, Practices, Activism and Utopias* series, launched in 2021, explores twenty-first-century movements that challenge the economic and political order of global capitalism by developing new cultures, new practices, and campaigning for alternative futures. In the turmoil of gross injustices, inequities, and ecosystem destruction, the series aims to offer clear analyses, proposals, and debates. This second book in the series offers a smorgasbord of analyses of where we are now and radical visions of post-capitalist futures where fair and just relationships and ecological sustainability are paramount.

Certain contributors have particular foci and address specific questions. What can we elicit about futures from the forces of right and left competing to persuade the majority of societal discontents? What are possible futures for Chinese state capitalism? Why is diversity significant, from a community economies perspective? How might we best define the appropriate uses and control of technology to drive more just and sustainable futures? Which ways are optimum to deal with exponential debts caused by falling output due to cuts in carbon emission and extensive investments needed to develop alternative energy supplies?

Other contributors explore deep system change. There are ecosocialist visions, from state-oriented and market-regulating plans for transformation to grassroots community modes of production networked across a pluriverse globe where market, money, and state dissolve into commoning and co-governance. Degrowth, which focuses on humanity living within Earth's limits in equitable and convivial ways, offers redistributive state policies and community-based economic initiatives that inspire—and are inspired by—cultural acceptance of material sufficiency versus exponential growth. Strong arguments are put for direct provision of universal basic services, incorporating participatory democracy and guaranteed work, rather than a market-oriented universal basic income scheme.

In contrast to a materials- and energy-hungry, technology-driven green new deal, a transformation based on core human-oriented and earth-centred infrastructure is proposed. In terms of advances for first peoples and addressing conditions wrought by global heating, there is a call for contemporary states to cede political autonomy and subsidiarity, for sentient landscapes to inspire as-it-were sentient economies—plural, hybrid economies. Renewal of cultural and ecological diversity, based on a politics and economics of localisation and resistance, with decentralisation and appropriate technologies joined up by international alliances and common principles offers a future imbued with the sacred.

Ecological justice triumphs in the case of a tiny South Indian town's struggle to stop Coca-Cola polluting and hogging their water supplies, a struggle that spreads like a pandemic to a national campaign and on to a manifesto on the universal right to access quality water. Significantly, the collection concludes with a collectively written intellectual massage drawing emotions and subjectivities and localities to the centre of practice.

In short, this collection offers an array of insights for those seeking inspiration in dark times, for reading and discussion groups, for undergraduates and academics in a range of fields. As Malcolm X said in 1962 'The future belongs to those who prepare for it today.'

Melbourne, VIC, Australia   Anitra Nelson
5 May 2021

Contents

1 **Introduction** 1
Samuel Alexander, Sangeetha Chandrashekeran, and Brendan Gleeson

Part I Alternative Paradigms for Post-Capitalist Futures 21

2 **The Race to Replace a Dying Neoliberalism** 23
Walden Bello

3 **Ecosocialism from a Post-Development Perspective** 31
Anitra Nelson

4 **Post-Capitalism Now: A Community Economies Approach** 41
Jenny Cameron

5 **Collective Sufficiency: Degrowth as a Political Project** 53
Samuel Alexander and Brendan Gleeson

6 **China: Capitalism and Change?** 65
Michael Webber

Part II Governing for Post-Capitalist Futures 75

7 **From Technological Utopianism to Universal Basic Services** 77
Boris Frankel

8 Ecofeminist Political Economy: Critical Reflections on the
   Green New Deal 87
   Christine Bauhardt

9 The Macroeconomics of Degrowth: Can Planned
   Economic Contraction Be Stable? 97
   Steve Keen

10 Post-Capitalist Techno-Futures: Beyond Instrumental
   Utopianism 107
   Sangeetha Chandrashekeran and Jathan Sadowski

11 Crises, COVID, and the Climate State 117
   Peter Christoff

Part III Post-Capitalist Geographies and Resistance 127

12 Localisation: The World Beyond Capitalism 129
   Helena Norberg-Hodge

13 Indigenous Australians and Their Lands: Post-Capitalist
   Development Alternatives 141
   Jon Altman

14 Environmental Justice Movements as Mediums of Post-
   Capitalist Futures: Perspectives from India 153
   Brototi Roy

15 Careful Thinking: Pensar Cuidando—Henvupen Yaconso 165
   Camila Marambio, Hema'ny Molina, and Bárbara Saavedra

Index 179

Notes on Contributors

Samuel Alexander is a lecturer and researcher at the University of Melbourne, Australia, teaching a course called 'Consumerism and the Growth Economy: Critical Interdisciplinary Perspectives' as part of the Master of Environment. He is also a research fellow at the Melbourne Sustainable Society Institute and co-director of the Simplicity Institute. Alexander's interdisciplinary research focuses on degrowth, permaculture, voluntary simplicity, 'grassroots' theories of transition, and the relationship between culture and political economy. His recent books (co-authored with Brendan Gleeson) include *Degrowth in the Suburbs* (2019) and *Urban Awakenings* (2020).

Jon Altman initially trained as a development economist then as an anthropologist. He has undertaken field-based research on Indigenous development alternatives in remote Australia for over four decades. His approach deploys the theoretical lenses of economic hybridity emphasising the resilience of non-capitalist production relations based on kinship and custom. He is currently an emeritus professor at the School of Regulation and Global Governance, The Australian National University, and a director of several not-for-profit organisations that support alternate development thinking, activism, and practice.

Christine Bauhardt is professor at Humboldt-Universität zu Berlin where she heads the division of Gender and Globalisation. She holds a

PhD in political science and wrote her second book on the theory and politics of spatial and environmental planning. Her latest publication is the edited volume *Feminist Political Ecology and the Economics of Care* (with Wendy Harcourt), published in the Routledge Studies in Ecological Economics series. Her work focuses on feminist economics, ecofeminism, queer ecologies, and environmental politics with a special interest in technical infrastructures.

Walden Bello is the co-founder of and current senior analyst at the Bangkok-based Focus on the Global South, and is International Adjunct Professor of Sociology at the State University of New York at Binghamton. He received the Right Livelihood Award, also known as the Alternative Nobel Prize, in 2003, and was named Outstanding Public Scholar of the International Studies Association in 2008. He is the author or co-author of 25 books, the latest of which is *Counterrevolution: The Global Rise of the Far Right* (2019). He served in the Philippines' House of Representatives from 2009 to 2015, during which time he was the chairman of that body's Committee on Overseas Workers' Affairs.

Jenny Cameron is a Conjoint Associate Professor in the Discipline of Geography and Environmental Studies at the University of Newcastle, Australia. She is currently Deputy Chair and Secretary of the Community Economies Institute and was a founding member of the Community Economies Research Network. As an activist and academic she has been involved in community, research, and teaching activities that shed light on the economic diversity that already exists in the world and that forms the basis for building post-capitalist worlds now.

Sangeetha Chandrashekeran is a geographer at the University of Melbourne. She is Deputy Director of the Melbourne Sustainable Society Institute and senior research fellow at the Centre of Excellence for Children and Families over the Life Course. Sangeetha's research examines issues of equity and justice in environmental change. She has focused on the energy transition in Australia and the role of the state in marketisation of the sector.

Peter Christoff is Senior Research Fellow with the Melbourne Climate Futures initiative and Associate Professor with the School of Geography at the University of Melbourne. His research focuses on Australian and international climate and environmental policy, and his books include *Globalisation and the Environment* (with Robyn Eckersley) (2013) and *Four Degrees of Global Warming: Australia in a Hot World* (2013).

Boris Frankel is Honorary Principal Fellow, Melbourne Institute of Sustainable Society, University of Melbourne. He is a long-established author, teacher, and media commentator. His most recent books are the trilogy *Fictions of Sustainability: The Politics of Growth and Post-Capitalist Futures* (2018), *Capitalism Versus Democracy? Rethinking Politics in the Age of Environmental Crisis* (2020), and *Democracy Versus Sustainability* (2021).

Brendan Gleeson is Professor of Urban Policy Studies and Director of the Melbourne Sustainable Society Institute at the University of Melbourne. He researches urban and social issues. His recent books, *Degrowth in the Suburbs* (2019) and *Urban Awakenings* (2020) were written with Samuel Alexander.

Steve Keen is Professor of Economics and Distinguished Research Fellow at the Institute for Strategy, Resilience and Security at University College London. A specialist in complex systems modelling in economics, he has publications on nonequilibrium macroeconomics, environmental economics, the role of energy in production, critiques of Neoclassical and Marxian economics, monetary dynamics, empirical data on causes of financial crises, and economic methodology. He is author of *Debunking Economics* (2001, 2011), *Can We Avoid Another Financial Crisis?* (2017), and *The New Economics: A Manifesto* (2021). He is also winner of the Revere Award for being the economist 'who first and most clearly anticipated and gave public warning of the Global Financial Collapse and whose work is most likely to prevent another GFC in the future'.

Camila Marambio (Papudo, Chile) is a curator and founded Ensayos in 2010 motivated by the strong sentiment that Tierra del Fuego is the centre of the world. Marambio holds a PhD in Curatorial Practice from Monash University, Naarm/Melbourne; an MA in Modern Art: Curatorial Studies from Columbia University, NYC; and a Master of Experiments in Art and Politics, Sciences Po, Paris. She is postdoctoral fellow at The Seedbox: A Mistra-Formas Environmental Humanities Collaboratory, Linkoping University, Sweden. She is co-author of the books *Slow Down*

Fast, A Toda Raja with Cecilia Vicuña (2019) and *Sandcastles: Cancer as Dangerous Talent* with Nina Lykke (forthcoming, 2022).

Hema'ny Molina (Santiago, Chile) is a Selk'nam writer, activist, craftswoman, and grandmother. Molina is president of the Selk'nam Corporation Chile, formed in 2015, which aims to dislodge the indigenous community from the stigma of 'extinction'. She is also a founding member of Hach Saye, a family-run Selk'nam cultural organisation.

Anitra Nelson is an activist scholar affiliated with the Melbourne Sustainable Society Institute, University of Melbourne. She is author of *Beyond Money: A Postcapitalist Strategy* (2022) and *Small is Necessary: Shared Living on a Shared Planet* (2018), co-author of *Exploring Degrowth: A Critical Guide* (2020), and co-editor of *Food for Degrowth: Perspectives and Practices* (2021) and *Housing for Degrowth: Principles, Models, Challenges and Opportunities* (2018).

Helena Norberg-Hodge is a pioneer of the new economy movement, and has been promoting an economics of personal, social, and ecological wellbeing for more than 40 years. She is a recipient of the Alternative Nobel Prize, the Arthur Morgan Award, and the Goi Peace Prize. Author of the inspirational classic *Ancient Futures*, she is also producer of the award-winning documentary *The Economics of Happiness*. Helena is the founder and director of Local Futures and The International Alliance for Localisation.

Brototi Roy researches environmental justice movements, with a focus on India, using the lens of ecological economics and political ecology. She has a PhD from the Institut de Ciencia i Tecnologia Ambientals, Universitat Autònoma de Barcelona (ICTA-UAB). She is the co-founder of *Degrowth India Initiative* and the current President-Elect of *Research&Degrowth*, the Barcelona-based collective on research and activism on degrowth.

Bárbara Saavedra (Santiago, Chile) is a biologist specialising in ecology and conservation and has been the director of the Wildlife Conservation Society (WCS) for Chile since 2005. Since then, she has led the implementation of a new science-based, multiple-scale, locally integrated, globally relevant conservation model at WCS Karukinka Natural Park. She received her PhD in Evolutionary Biology from the University of Chile. She is director of the Ecological Society of Chile and member of the Civil Society Council of Institute of Human Rights of Chile, where she connects her vision of justice with biodiversity conservation. As a member of the eco-feminist collective Ensayos, she raises the voice of conservation and ecology beyond NGOs. Her advocacy successes at WCS include the protection of 70,000 hectares of peatlands through the Chilean Ministry of Mining and the declaration of the Admiralty Sound as a Marine Protected Area.

Jathan Sadowski is a research fellow in the Emerging Technologies Research Lab in the Faculty of Information Technology, as well as in the Data Program of the ARC Centre of Excellence for Automated Decision-Making and Society, both at Monash University. His work studies the political economy of technology, labour, and capital. He is the author of *Too Smart: How Digital Capitalism is Extracting Data, Controlling our Lives, and Taking Over the World* (2020).

Michael Webber is Professor Emeritus in the School of Geography, Earth and Atmospheric Sciences, University of Melbourne. An economic geographer by training, he has spent the last several decades conducting research in and on China, with a specific focus on environmental management during the emergence of capitalism. His recent books include *Making Capitalism in Rural China* (2012) and (with Jon Barnett and others) *Water Supply in a Mega-City* (2018). He is currently the lead investigator on a large research project about Chinese hydropolitics.

List of Figures

Fig. 4.1	The Diverse Economies Iceberg. (Source: Diverse Economies Iceberg by Community Economies Collective is licensed under a Creative Commons Attribution-ShareAlike 4.0 International License. Available from https://www.communityeconomies.org/resources/diverse-economies-iceberg)	43
Fig. 9.1	The relationship between change in energy and change in GDP	100
Fig. 9.2	The 2008 crisis left the USA and the world with the highest private debt levels in history	102
Fig. 13.1	Aboriginal titled lands and discrete Indigenous communities in 2020. (Data sources: Altman and Markham (2015) updated by Dr Francis Markham with information from the 2016 Census and the National Native Title Tribunal http://www.nntt.gov.au/Maps/Determinations_map.pdf, accessed 3 June 2020)	144

1

Introduction

Samuel Alexander, Sangeetha Chandrashekeran, and Brendan Gleeson

Covid Contradictions

We write this introduction in the middle of 2021, in the midst of the COVID-19 pandemic causing so much human suffering and disruption. This seems to be the beginning of a new crisis-ridden period in socio-environmental history whose duration and lasting impact are impossible to forecast. We editors certainly won't pretend to fully understand what is happening. None of us can foresee how this crisis will finally unfold and what changes it will bring to the world, including its political economy, which for decades has been firmly framed by the diktat of neoliberal globalisation.

The social, economic, and political trauma caused by the pandemic further erodes the legitimacy of capitalism as the hegemonic mode of social and economic organisation. To be sure, there has been prolonged speculation and dispute about this broad critique, but the current

---

S. Alexander (✉) • S. Chandrashekeran • B. Gleeson
Melbourne Sustainable Society Institute, University of Melbourne, Parkville, VIC, Australia
e-mail: sangeetha.chandra@unimelb.edu.au; brendan.gleeson@unimelb.edu.au

disruptions which the virus has elicited add further burdens to what was already an unstable system. The crises of care that this pandemic has laid bare—both of people and planet—are not new, but they have been highlighted by it, the contradictions deepening and increasingly resistant to resolution within the existing order.

The latest violent and disruptive manifestations of the virus are neither new nor more significant than what has gone before. Capitalism has driven rounds of dispossession and violence in recent centuries, beginning with colonialism and imperialism dating from the fifteenth century (Mamdani 2020) and exacerbated by the Industrial Revolution and the current carbon age. For much of the world, especially those in the Global South or marginalised groups in the Global North, the trauma of capitalism was always and already present, and is being played out in the new coronavirus context. A feature of the onset of the virus in the early stages was its indiscriminate path of contagion—a shock to affluent societies who have largely managed to buy their way to good health through expensive high-tech interventions and salubrious environments. We now know that exposure to the virus can be limited through the privilege of wealth (staying safe and comfortable in a private dwelling with secure tenure and secure working conditions etc.). And the great hope of vaccination is unevenly distributed, reflecting the well-established fault lines of uneven development and inequity. As we write, 80% of vaccines have gone to those in high- or upper-middle-income countries and 0.2% to those in low-income countries (Bello 2021). In India, where the virus is raging, only 2% of the population has been fully vaccinated as of May 2021. Coronavirus provides yet another case study of capitalism's deep contradictions.

Capitalism and Its Discontents

A book on post-capitalist futures must begin by summarising the constitutive elements of capitalism whilst recognising the risks and limitations of any singular or static definition. This involves crafting a narrative that is alert to essentialist tendencies and eschews the illusion of inevitability (see Block 2019), but also develops a basic foundation—a terra firma out of, or against which, new futures can unfold. To do this we begin with a rejection of the economy as an autonomous self-organising system subject to immutable laws, and favour a view of economies as socially embedded and governed in and through politics. Capitalism refers to assemblages of social relations that include but are not reducible to the following: private property rights and possessive individualism; the privileged role of the market and commodification processes; growth-oriented logics geared towards accumulation; and the exploitation along class, gender/sexuality, and racial lines and resulting inequalities.

Capitalism coexists and co-evolves with a range of histories and geographies. Core logics and processes are animated through diverse contexts and spatial differences. We embrace Jamie Peck's articulation of capitalist variegation which '… speaks to a kind of genetic variation, to moving mutations and matrices realized across sites and scales, and to open horizons, both analytically and politically, rather than clunky concepts or foreclosed futures' (Peck 2019: 5). It is the potential indeterminacy and the possibility of alternative futures emerging in and out of capitalist hegemony that this edited collection seeks to explore. Each chapter in this volume can be understood as examining one or more of these constitutive elements of capitalism, considering what might emerge if those elements were removed or significantly transformed. Capitalist relations may never fully disappear from our world in the foreseeable future, but what if varieties of post-capitalist relations came to transform existing political economies through social and political action?

Capitalism is a political economy that, after centuries of incubation during the feudal era, achieved a certain coherence in logic and form in Europe during the eighteenth century. Raymond Williams (1983) believed that the word 'capitalism' was first used in Europe in the early years of the nineteenth century. The capitalist order later spread through Europe's 'neworlds' aided greatly by the violent appropriations of competitive imperialism and colonialism. By the mid-nineteenth century it had already adopted a totalising global ambition. Capital's relentless compulsion for expansion was noted by Marx and Engels in *The Communist Manifesto* of 1848 (Kamenka 1983: 207): 'The need of a constantly expanding market for its products chases the bourgeoisie over the whole surface of the globe. It must nestle everywhere, settle everywhere, establish connexions everywhere…it creates a world after its own image.'

This remaking of the world continued apace during the twentieth century, disturbed but never halted by the great perturbations—depression, fascism, war, and genocide—that it helped to create. There were resistances and countercurrents, most notably the assertion of socialist orders in specific parts of the globe outside the 'Western sphere'. By the late twentieth century, however, these alternative political economies had largely foundered (with the qualified exception of China), thus releasing vast final territories for capitalist annexation.

In the first fifth of the twenty-first century, capitalism, at all levels, global to local, has manifested what Wolfgang Streeck in his recent writings—notably *Buying Time* (2014) and an essay 'How Will Capitalism End?' (2014b: 64)—calls 'five worsening disorders for which no cure is at hand: declining growth, oligarchy, starvation of the public sphere, corruption and international anarchy'. We would add the mounting crises in and of natural systems upon which capitalism depends. Although the destabilising decline of global ecosystems and biodiversity doesn't feature strongly in Streeck's work, he acknowledges that global warming and biospheric collapse are certain to intensify these terminal disorders. The deepening contradictions of capitalism, as well as its declining social legitimacy, are such that even those on the Left who have traditionally taken the mortal not morbid view of contemporary capitalism—for example, David Harvey (2014)—are now persuaded that the system faces seemingly insurmountable contradictions that will force its retrenchment and radical reconfiguration.

Perhaps it is merely liberal democracy that is at peril? Streeck (2014a: 64) maintains that 'capitalism's shotgun marriage with democracy since 1945 is breaking up'. This union may be coming to an end but perhaps the former doesn't need the latter for its survival? Capital could resort to its fine inner machinery to secure its future. History records this possibility, notably in the rise in Europe of corporatism and fascism in the early decades of the twentieth century, where an alliance of monopoly capitals and weaponised states was able to suspend democracy without halting accumulation. In the present conjuncture, Streeck sees the ascendancy of oligarchs, especially but not only in former socialist countries, as signalling this possibility anew. On the ground, rising right-wing populism threatens to undermine the machinery of democracy not the work of capital (Kapferer and Theodossopoulos 2019).

In this time of virus management the possibility for boldly advancing authoritarianism is certainly evident—perhaps signalled in the strong state responses authorised by the struggle to control the pandemic. But neither Streeck nor Harvey offers even a sketch outline for what dispensation is likely to replace capitalism as it continues its catabolic collapse. With this in mind, the work of imagining and essaying existing and emergent alternative social forms seems a compelling and urgent duty for radical and responsible thinkers.

Future Imaginaries and Imaginary Futures

Such labours have produced this volume, which throws searchlights in quest of post-capitalist futures. The brief we editors set contributors was an open one, freed from the restraints of traditional thinking which has fixed socialism and communism, or any Marxian prescription, as the inevitable successor(s) to capitalism. Such radical thinking, insightful as it has been, has not fully or consistently comprehended the ways in which ecological and socio-cultural forces might condition the potentially myriad societal forms that could emerge if or when capitalism submerges into history.

Of course, there are vast literatures in the feminist and non-Western academic-activist tradition that imagine radical futures and engage in practices of re-worlding. Donna Haraway's (2016) work inspires us to build more liveable futures together on a damaged Earth by embracing diverse modes of (multispecies) sociality. 'Re-worlding' involves imagining a pluriversal world where 'many worlds fit' and grounding this in respect for Indigenous sustainability sciences, local self-managing cultures, ethics of care and nurture, and a celebration of cultural difference (Salleh 2020). For Silvia Rivera Cusicanqui, the Andean concept of *ch'ixi* provides an alternative to binary thinking, refusing to resolve into a certain path, but instead living in and celebrating the contradiction, experiencing the risky and creative edges for planetary living (see Gálvez 2019). For others, like J.K. Gibson-Graham, it is not so much about imaginary distant futures, but magnifying the radical alternatives or 'community economies' of the present moment that can be nurtured and expanded into the future (Gibson-Graham 2006). Bottom-up social movements like *Buen Vivir* and *Swaraj* and Zapatista resistance enact radical alternatives in real time and spaces. Recent edited collections on post-development elaborate diverse alternative futures and have been a source of inspiration for this book (see Kothari et al. 2019; Klein and Morreo 2019).

These are the creative, imaginative, and radical frontiers of post-capitalist futures. Much of this work interrogates the universalist temporalities that underpin capitalism's dominance and frame the terms of reference for opposition. Capitalist futures are embedded in an ontology of modernist Time that fetishises the mechanistic workings of clocks and calendars. This produces a linear concept of *before* and *after* that can be deployed to coordinate and discipline in accordance with the goals of economic production (Kolinjivadi et al. 2019). The universalisation of modernist Time situates 'man' (sic) as the motive force governing and shaping a distinct and separate sphere of 'nature' through modes of learning, knowing, engineering, etc. Even as capitalism's endless quest for expansion drives socio-ecological crises threatening its very survival, the linear temporality is reinforced through the search for new triumphant futures that can overcome such crises (and reap a profit!). These techno-utopian fixes will be dwarfed by the realities and temporalities of tipping points. As ecological thresholds are crossed, there is no return to 'normal', and drastic socio-ecological impacts accelerate and intensify particularly for those with the least responsibility and power to adjust.

While much of the post-capitalist literature hones in on the problems of growth and critiques the exploitative nature of capitalist relations, it rarely engages with and interrogates the socionatural temporalities that underpin capitalism's dominance. Instead, post-capitalist explorers often deploy a universalist temporality—a key epistemological tool of capitalist oppression—but put this in service of preferred objectives: to live well, to care, to common, etc. This licences certain forms of political imagination (revolution, reform, de/recentralisation) whilst devaluing imaginaries that are fundamentally incompatible with the notion of linear futures. This includes messy, non-linear lifeworlds that are co-produced through human and non-human agency; relationships and connectivities that cannot be coordinated in time but are instead unpredictable, incalculable, and emergent; pedagogies of observation and deep listening not in control; and logics and ethics of care that are responsive to the local seasonal rhythms of growing, becoming, and passing away.

This book contains a variety of future imaginaries, amongst which there is a degree of contradiction and counter proposition. We welcome this diversity as it was our intention to create a work where post-capitalist futures are richly conceived not narrowly ordained. As capitalist crises continue to deepen and intensify, further disruptions lie in our collective future, a future at once common but always differentiated. In words attributed to fiction writer William Gibson: the future is already here, it is just unevenly distributed. Which of those already-existing post-capitalist futures will or should come to dominate? Where will they dominate? What will drive them into existence? And whose or which interests will they serve?

These are some of the questions raised and explored in this book, all of them haunted by the fact that capitalism, albeit in a condition of seemingly fatal deterioration, does not seem to be dissolving without a fierce struggle. It remains as a monarch, albeit on a crumbling throne. We fear a violent and destructive ending to the rule of the market. The task of imagining better futures, and the means to secure them peaceably, is an urgency running through the pages of this collection. In short, our volume seeks to position itself beyond capitalist realism.

Beyond Capitalist Realism

'Capitalist realism' is a term popularised by the late British political theorist Mark Fisher, in a provocative and unsettling book by that name (Fisher 2009). The term implies that ever since the fall of Soviet Communism in 1989, capitalism has been the only game in town, the only *realistic* system of production, distribution, and consumption to structure globalised human society. Everything else is sheer utopianism in the pejorative sense—naïve dreaming of what can never be. In a phrase that has almost become a cliché, capitalist realism points to a failure of imagination, suggesting that it is now easier to imagine the end of the world than the end of capitalism. As one looks around the world today, the depth of capitalism's entrenchment in the global order is, admittedly, difficult to deny, as Fisher himself was the first to admit, even as he resisted it. It can tempt one to despair, for it often seems that there is in fact no realistic alternative to ecocidal capitalism.

The editors of this book have never subscribed to capitalist realism, even though it is clear that capitalist realism reflects the *zeitgeist* of the twenty-first century. It is a perspective shared not only by neoliberal conservatives but also by most on the green-left, who, despite a 'progressive' self-image, remain insidiously entrenched in capitalism's growth paradigm. In Fisher's words, there is 'a widespread sense that not only is capitalism the only viable political and economic system, but also that it is now impossible even to *imagine* a coherent alternative to it' (Fisher 2009: 2). What has emerged is a 'business ontology', according to which 'it is *simply obvious* that everything in society, including healthcare and education, should be run as a business' (Fisher 2009: 17).

Fisher describes this consciousness as a 'pervasive atmosphere' that conditions 'not only the production of culture but also the regulation of work and education, and acting as a kind of invisible barrier constraining thought and action' (Fisher 2009: 16). But here is the disturbing paradox of capitalist realism: just as the dominant cultural imagination has contracted into a singularity of vision—there is no alternative to capitalism!—the very system to which there is apparently no alternative shows itself to be in the process of self-destructing, like a cancer cell growing itself to death, killing its host. Indeed, the ease with which 'small government' advocates have shifted to Keynesian pump priming particularly on social service expenditure in response to the pandemic shows how quickly this pervasive atmosphere can abate, paradoxically in the quest to save capitalism.

What can we expect during the period of system retrenchment? Streeck (2014a: 64) writes: 'On the basis of capitalism's recent historical record … a long and painful period of cumulative decay: of intensifying frictions, of fragility and uncertainty, and of a steady succession of "normal accidents'". In other words, a period of intensifying and transformative violence. The relentless pessimism of these prognoses, whilst underpinned by critical realism, can foreclose more productive debates about alternative futures and what ought to come next. Rather than focusing on the morbid symptoms that appear in that space as the old dies while the new cannot yet be born, this edited collection seeks to orient itself beyond the carnage towards a horizon of possibility with 'hope without optimism' (Eagleton 2015).

We maintain that capitalist realism is unrealistic, non-viable, a dead end—literally. The global economic system is full of internal contradictions that it cannot resolve, most notably the myth that through market mechanisms and 'techno-fixes' we can purchase and consume our way to sustainability. Vast oceans of debilitating poverty surround small oceans of unfathomable plenty, exposing the violent betrayal of the capitalist growth agenda (Piketty 2014; Hickel 2017). This is a race leading towards an abyss, both enabled and entrenched by this sterility of imagination Fisher called capitalist realism. Fortunately—if that is the right word—capitalist realism 'can only be threatened if it is shown to be in some way inconsistent or untenable; if, that is to say, capitalism's ostensible "realism" turns out to be nothing of the sort' (Fisher 2009: 16).

Of course, as history relates, capitalism is a dexterous beast, always shifting and changing with the times to exploit new opportunities for profit and in response to new challenges to its legitimacy. Nevertheless, the overlapping range of ecological, social, financial, and health crises indicate that, one way or another, the coming years and decades will see growing pressure on the global capitalist system and the emergence of new political and economic forms and imaginaries. As crises deepen and intensify, a descent or rupture of some form approaches, with further ecological, technological, and social realities destined to disrupt (already disrupting) the status quo. The pandemic is just one more nail in the coffin of late-stage capitalism. The human challenge is to ensure that the post-capitalist era emerges as far as possible through design rather than disaster.

Accordingly, this book rejects capitalist realism as unrealistic, as an artefact of false consciousness, blind to its ecocidal nature. Technology cannot save capitalism from its cannibalistic nature nor will the so-called 'trickle down' effect resolve the deep injustices of its colonial and patriarchal past and present. And no Green New Deal will contribute much to a 'just transition' if it remains hooked on to an extractivist economics of growth which a finite planet evidently cannot bear. Thinking and acting 'beyond capitalism' is not easy in a world governed by a one-dimensional ideology that is increasingly homogenised, commodified, and standardised, yet breaking through the cracks of capitalism to think otherwise and be otherwise is more essential now than ever. In the words of Herman Hesse: 'Nothing is harder, yet nothing is more necessary, than to speak of certain things whose existence is neither demonstrable nor probable. The very fact that serious and conscientious people treat them as existing things brings them a step closer to existence and to the possibility of being born' (Hesse 1972).

Contemplating a Crisis-Ridden Exit from Capitalism

There is no reason to believe that the current season of forced economic contraction represents a permanent and final dislocation of the growth machine ambitions of capitalist globalisation. As this book goes to print, the old engine seems to be spluttering back into action. The relatively recent experience of the Global Financial Crisis (GFC) (2008–2009) and its aftermath is a worrying precedent. There was much joyous banging of cymbals and song from progressive interests as Keynesian desiderata were rediscovered and reapplied. The revealed downside of this reinstatement of 'progress' was a failure to grasp that Keynes' theories predated political ecology and were intended to rescue, not transform, industrial capitalism. Hence, the way out of the GFC crisis was a massive re-stimulation of overconsumption and all the ecological destruction that goes with it. After a major dip, carbon emissions quickly accelerated and, after some mild disturbance, the planet set back on its path for climate destruction. The shadow of Keynes lay heavy on the refiring smokestack economies of the world.

We fear this replay for the current crisis—our anxieties deepened by the observation earlier that capitalism is a particularly historically insentient animal. The forces willing for a 'snap back' are immense, throughout the Global North. It's easy to highlight, not to say pillory, the 'let's re-open for business' cant of ex-President Trump, but as Streeck reminds us, the European Union is a deeply neoliberal institution, essentially a free trade bloc, that is equally committed in the current historical moment to the earliest possible resumption of the growth machine. The centre-Left and green parties typically operate within the same growth paradigm, too often committed to little more than a limp 'third way' that 'regulates the market' and talks of 'greening capitalism' or giving it a human face. We suggest that that is merely going down the wrong road more slowly.

But caution is advised. The cloak of pessimism is too often the disguise of determinism, a tendency that we reject as bad science and politics. Both defeats and victories are snapped from the jaws of historical crises and it's far too early now to say what will come from the pandemic disruption. Still, if public discourse is anything to go by, it seems the primary goal of politics in this time of instability is to facilitate a 'bounce back' to where we were before the pandemic. Of course, all the evidence suggests that bouncing back would be no solution at all. We must not bounce back. We must bounce otherwise, forward and elsewhere (Wright 2010).

In this historical moment, then, can we contemplate a crisis-driven exit from capitalism? As Fisher (2009: 80–81) maintained: 'The very pervasiveness of capitalist realism means that even glimmers of alternative political and economic possibilities can have a disproportionately great effect. The tiniest event can tear a hole in the grey curtain of reaction which has marked the horizons of possibility under capitalist realism. From a situation in which nothing can happen, suddenly anything is possible again.' The point is that the instability induced by the pandemic is already looking like a time of radical opening in thought and action. Even the neoliberals are shifting ground and rhetoric. For now, all we can do is nod approvingly at the words degrowth scholar Jason Hickel recently cast out into cyberspace: 'Capitalist realism is over. Everything is thinkable.'

We trust that this book will contribute to this growing sense of *capitalist unrealism*—to a conviction that viable and desirable alternatives to capitalism exist, alternatives that are in the process of being lived into existence by the collective rumbling of social movements that are bubbling everywhere under the surface and on the streets of the existing order. What is clear is that humanity has not arrived at the 'end of history', as Francis Fukuyama once famously declared—for history is always and everywhere just beginning.

Post-Capitalist Futures

A book on post-capitalist futures should be infinite in scope, an open-ended series of story-telling and world-making exercises reflecting the inherently pluriversal possibilities of our existence. Unfortunately, the exigencies of commercial publishing and mainstream academic life have limited this to 14 short chapters. As a result, numerous themes that could rightfully claim space in an edited collection of this nature have not found their way in. This includes important critical perspectives from science-fiction that allow us to conjure otherwise unimaginable futures; more-than-emergent financial futures of cryptocurrencies and algorithm-based trade; futures developed through trial and error in worker cooperatives or ecovillages; and small and large-scale experiments in market socialism, participatory economics, or peer-to-peer networking and exchange. We acknowledge these limitations and more, but at the same time are determined to showcase a selection of perspectives that are organised around the themes of alternative paradigms, governing futures, and geographies of resistance. We now offer a short overview of each chapter.

Part I: Alternative Paradigms for Post-Capitalist Futures

The opening section of the book presents various alternative paradigms for thinking about—and working toward—post-capitalist futures. Chapter 2 conjures Gramsci by putting politics, ideology, and the strategies of mobilisation at the centre of the post-capitalist imaginary.

In 'The Race to Replace a Dying Neoliberalism', Walden Bello analyses the space opened up by the destabilising coronavirus pandemic, exploring various futures that might now lie ahead for humanity, both in the Global North and the Global South. He argues that the world was still recovering from the Global Financial Crisis of 2008–2009 when the pandemic landed, exacerbating neoliberal capitalism's ideological crisis of legitimacy. A struggle has now ensued between progressive alternatives and the authoritarian far right, with the latter having more success mobilising politically to date than the former. Nevertheless, Bello refuses to count out the left in this battle for ideological and political hegemony. He acknowledges that progressives have rich and coherent visions for a post-neoliberal organisation of economic life, the challenge being to translate these into a critical mass via political organising.[1]

Socialism is arguably the primary anti-capitalist tradition and alternative framing. In Chap. 3, 'Ecosocialism from a Post-development Perspective', Anitra Nelson examines post-capitalist futures through the lens of ecosocialism. She shows how in recent decades socialism has been enriched by various post-growth and post-development literatures that have sought to respond to today's worsening socio-ecological predicament (see Kothari et al. 2019; Klein and Morreo 2019). Nelson analyses two prominent tensions in this emerging movement for ecosocialism. The first relates to theories of transition, with some ecosocialists arguing that the driving forces for change must come from the state via 'top down' structural interventions, while others argue that an ecosocialist society must or should be driven into existence by grassroots activists working 'from below'. The second tension that is highlighted concerns the varying degrees that markets and money are featured in differing ecosocialist traditions. Nelson contends that post-development conceptions of ecosocialism challenge capitalism most directly.

The search for alternative futures can sometimes obscure the political-economic diversity that already exists, further marginalising these alternatives each time the world is referred to as capitalist. In Chap. 4, 'Post-Capitalism Now: A Community Economies Perspective', Jenny Cameron draws on and develops the pioneering work of J.K. Gibson-Graham to present a

---

[1] A revised version of Bello's chapter first appeared in *Foreign Policy in Focus* on 13 May 2020. We are grateful for this opportunity to republish.

'community economies' perspective of post-capitalism. This scholarship recognises that there is a diversity of economic activities and relationships that are not capitalist and that are not necessarily subsumed to capitalist dynamics (see also, Wright 2010). Cameron uses examples from a range of urban contexts to illustrate how post-capitalism is not something to be conjured in the future but is already here. She articulates and defends a strategy that calls on activists to work with others to help strengthen the economic activities and relationships that are already enacting the post-capitalist worlds that so many of us yearn for.

In Chap. 5, 'Collective Sufficiency: Degrowth as a Political Project', Samuel Alexander and Brendan Gleeson argue for a degrowth paradigm of planned economic contraction for overdeveloped capitalist nations. This is proposed as the only coherent way to resolve the existential threat of ecological overshoot and address the failures of 'green growth' and 'technofix' approaches. They maintain that capitalism is a mode of political economy that is proving unable to resolve the ecological and financial crises that it produces, suggesting that the future will be post-capitalist, whether by design or disaster. The distributive implications of degrowth are highlighted to ensure social justice and wellbeing during economic contraction. Like Cameron, they highlight the role grassroots social movements and alternative economic experiments might need to play in prefiguring degrowth economies and creating the cultural conditions for a politics and macroeconomics of degrowth to emerge.

For decades China has presented as the pre-eminent challenge to capitalist realism, providing an example at times of 'actually existing socialism' and arguably a real-world alternative to capitalism. In Chap. 6, 'China: Capitalism and Change?', Michael Webber disabuses readers of any oversimplification or binary thinking by arguing that China's economy sits largely within, not beyond, the capitalist mode of production and distribution. These dynamics will be difficult to escape for various economic, cultural, political, and geopolitical reasons that are outlined. Webber argues there are several possible futures for China: soft authoritarian capitalism, perhaps with market-led pro-environment policies; state-dominated organisation of large-scale production, perhaps with state-led ecological modernisation; and a dystopian future that involves calamities more serious than the future of capitalism.

These diverse offerings in Part I attest to new forms of realism. We can call them 'radical realisms' that refuse the domineering assertions of the wounded capitalist order without underestimating the challenges facing movements for fundamental change.

Part II: Governing for Post-Capitalist Futures

The second section of the book offers various perspectives on alternative governance strategies and approaches for post-capitalist futures.

In Chap. 7, 'From Technological Utopianism to Universal Basic Services', Boris Frankel critically examines some of the most prominent currents in contemporary post-capitalist literature, including forecasts of a 'zero marginal cost' economy and arguments for a Universal Basic Income (UBI). Frankel highlights tensions in these technological utopian futures and argues that a more coherent post-capitalist vision emerges from the policy of Universal Basic Services (UBS). This policy would minimise the role of capitalist markets in determining societal pathways and distributive outcomes, and could help facilitate radical transitions to a degrowth or ecosocialist society.

Christine Bauhardt explores what role policies for a Green New Deal (GND) might need to play in the transition to a just and sustainable post-capitalist society. In Chap. 8, 'Ecofeminist Political Economy: Critical Reflections on the Green New Deal', Bauhardt draws on insights from ecofeminist political economy to show that social reproduction must be considered if both gender justice and ecological justice are to be achieved. Bauhardt also exposes how most framings of the GND remain entrenched in the unsustainable growth imperatives of capitalism—a growth paradigm that must be abandoned, she argues, if a GND is to achieve its social goals and genuinely be considered 'green'.

Steve Keen takes on the shibboleths of green growth by focusing on the limits to growth in energy. In Chap. 9, 'The Macroeconomics of Degrowth: Can Planned Economic Contraction Be Stable?' he argues that the growth paradigm of capitalism has energetic foundations, exemplified by the close correlation between GDP growth and energy use globally. But what if swift decarbonisation consistent with shrinking carbon budgets means that those abundant energy foundations are not available going forward? And what happens to debt if expected growth trajectories required to meet financial commitments prove non-viable? He examines a tradeable price mechanism whereby the burden of income reduction falls on the rich rather than the poor. At the same time, he maintains that we need to avoid past private sector financial commitments crippling the post-carbon economy, via a 'Modern Debt Jubilee'. Keen's view is that financing both proposals can be achieved using the insights of Modern Monetary Theory.

Organised labour and class politics—key engines for post-capitalist transformation in the Marxist literature—remain a somewhat underestimated quantity over the last few decades as capital has come to dominate and subjugate in new and creative ways. In Chap. 10, Sangeetha Chandrashekeran and Jathan Sadowski challenge futurist visions of the tech sector based on principles of Democratic Governance, Worker Power, Socially Beneficial Production, and Meaningful Labour. They argue that post-capitalist visions must be engaged with the current struggles and conditions of exploitation and informed by principles of resistance to the modes of capitalist exploitation.

Peter Christoff turns our attention to another core concern of the Marxist literature—the state. He examines the transformation of the political state through today's crises of the climate emergency and the coronavirus pandemic. In Chap. 11, 'Crises, COVID, and the Climate State', Christoff outlines how over the last 50 years most developed industrial countries have been marked by a transition from the welfare state to the neoliberal state. Writing during a time of pandemic, Christoff argues that we now have varieties of 'COVID capitalism', where core neoliberal political and economic conceptions have had to be set aside, perhaps permanently, to manage population health and mitigate spiralling unemployment. The crisis of climate change has to be set and interpreted in the context of these broader crises that envelop us, because they deepen the climate predicament in various ways. The financial burden of managing broader crises and demographic shifts make funding climate mitigation and adaptation even more challenging, and this squeezing of the public purse, among other things, is in the process of transforming the political sphere into what Christoff calls 'the Climate State'.

Part II's authors assert that there is an alternative radical reading to the term governance, usually taken by the left to mean a weakened, often privatised form of government. It accords with the view of radical prophet Ivan Illich, who saw a need to reinstate social politics in a technocratically possessed capitalism. Radical governances can emerge to bind a new marriage of democracy and an ecosocialised economy.

Part III: Post-Capitalist Geographies and Resistance

In the final section of the book, we have gathered various analyses of post-capitalist geographies and resistance. This section recognises the variegated nature of capitalism and therefore the variegated modes of opposition and re-worlding that are needed for effective resistance and future-building. There is a strong focus on local forms of agency that produce multiple, creative modes of social relations that challenge the dominance of capitalist logics and practices. The edited collection concludes with these accounts of post-capitalist futures already being enacted in place.

In Chap. 12, 'Localisation: The World Beyond Capitalism', Helena Norberg-Hodge presents a case that post-capitalist futures will need to be defined by highly localised and diverse economies. The key structural changes towards localisation that are discussed relate to land and farming; post-global business; finance and money; post-consumerism; reducing energy consumption; and reigning in techno-fetishism. In creating local economies from within globalised capitalism, Norberg-Hodge calls for a two-pronged approach of resistance and renewal. She argues that we need to both oppose the political forces driving further corporate domination, and actively create—or protect—a multiplicity of living, localised alternatives that can provide genuine material needs and social wellbeing while respecting and enhancing ecological diversity.

In Chap. 13, 'Indigenous Australians and their Lands: Post-Capitalist Development Alternatives', Jon Altman focuses on post-capitalist development alternatives that are already emerging in remote Australia for

Indigenous peoples who have repossessed their ancestral lands. His analysis is grounded in the notion of 'economic hybridity' that highlights the resilience and continuity of customary non-capitalist relations of production in remote Indigenous Australia. He also illustrates how, through their agency, Indigenous landowners are creatively reconfiguring and recombining elements of capitalist and non-capitalist forms of production. This theorisation challenges the envisioning of capitalism as the singular dominant mode of economy and might yet prove a harbinger of post-capitalist futures essential for Indigenous and non-Indigenous survival.

In Chap. 14, 'Environmental Justice Movements as Mediums of Post-Capitalist Futures: Perspectives from India', Brototi Roy offers a brief history of India's environmental justice movements and highlights some of the injustices that drive them. After a meta-review of such movements based on data from the Environmental Justice Atlas, Roy presents a case study of one resistance movement against a Coca-Cola bottling plant in the South Indian state of Kerala and the post-capitalist visions it encompassed. She concludes with insights from an Adivasi activist and poet on what is understood as 'real' development, which implies a decolonising approach. Roy highlights how this contrasts radically with capitalist conceptions of development and progress.

Chapter 15, 'Careful Thinking—Pensar Cuidando—Henvupen Yaconso', is co-authored by Camila Marambio (*Ensayos*), Hema'ny Molina (*Selk'nam*), Bárbara Saavedra (*WCS Chile*), who write collaboratively about the Patagonian peatbogs. The peatbogs have been degraded and continue to be endangered by numerous practices related to careless thinking. The authors link the exploitation of the Fuegian peatbog to the colonisation of the First Nations' Selk'nam peoples through state-sanctioned extermination policies. Repudiating the narrative of extinction, the authors compose a multi-vocal score that imagines futures of conservation, self-determination, and care. The practice of thinking and writing together makes visible the epistemological challenges of imagining post-capitalist, conserved futures, and performs the emancipatory practices of re-valuing, reclaiming, and re-visioning local sites.

We anticipate that these chapters will stimulate reimaginings beyond capitalist realism, whether they be optimistic or pessimistic futures, and add conceptual insights into the strategies needed to go beyond this assumed orthodoxy. Critical engagement with technological change, labour and class relations, and the changing nature of the state are necessary to conjure realistic and inspirational alternative futures. It is also important to recognise the already existing practices of communities as points of connection and continuity with the futures we seek to build. Our primary motivation in producing this collection was to challenge and inspire readers to think and act upon the pluriversal possibilities immanent in our crisis-ridden present.

References

Bello, Walden. 2021. The West Has Been Hoarding More Than Vaccines. *New York Times*, May 3.

Block, Fred. 2019. Problems with the Concept of Capitalism in the Social Sciences. *EPA: Economy and Space* 51 (5): 1–12.

Eagleton, Terry. 2015. *Hope Without Optimism*. New Haven: Yale University Press.

Fisher, Mark. 2009. *Capitalist Realism: Is There No Alternative?* Winchester: Zero Books.

Gálvez, Sarita. 2019. *A Quipu of the Chilean Chair in Post-Pinochet Chile: Propositions Towards South-South Pedagogical Possibilities*. PhD Monash, Melbourne.

Gibson-Graham, J.K. 2006. *Post Capitalist Politics*. Minneapolis: University of Minnesota Press.

Haraway, Donna. 2016. *Staying with the Trouble: Making Kin in the Chthulucene*. Durham: Duke University Press.

Harvey, David. 2014. *Seventeen Contradictions and the End of Capitalism*. Oxford University Press.

Hesse, Herman. 1972. *The Glass Bead Game*. London: Penguin Books.

Hickel, Jason. 2017. *The Divide: A Brief Guide to Global Inequality and its Solutions*. Cornerstone: William Heinemann.

Kamenka, Eugene, ed. 1983. *The Portable Marx*. London: Penguin.

Kapferer, Bruce, and Dimitrios Theodossopoulos, eds. 2019. *Democracy's Paradox: Populism and its Contemporary Crisis*. New York: Berghahn.

Klein, Elise, and Carlos Eduardo Morreo, eds. 2019. *Postdevelopment in Practice: Alternatives, Economies, Ontologies*. London: Routledge.

Kolinjivadi, Vijay, Diana Vela Almeida, and Jonathan Martineau. 2019. Can the Planet Really be Saved in Time? On the Temporalities of Socionature, the Clock and the Limits Debate. *Environment and Planning E: Nature and Space*. https://doi.org/10.1177/2514848619891874.

Kothari, Ashish, Ariel Salleh, Arturo Escobar, Federico Demaria, and Alberto Acosta, eds. 2019. *Pluriverse: A Post-Development Dictionary*. New York: Columbia University Press.

Mamdani, Mahmood. 2020. *Neither Settler nor Native: The Making and Unmaking of Permanent Minorities*. Cambridge, MA: Harvard University Press.

Peck, Jamie. 2019. Problematizing Capitalism(s): Big Differences? *EPA: Economy and Space* 51 (5): 1–7.

Piketty, Thomas. 2014. *Capital in the Twenty-First Century*. Cambridge: Harvard University Press.

Salleh, Ariel. 2020. Re-worlding—With a Pluriversal New Deal. *Arena Quarterly* No. 4, December. https://arena.org.au/re-worlding-with-a-pluriversal-new-deal/. Accessed 10 Feb 2021.

Streeck, Wolfgang. 2014a. How Will Capitalism End? *New Left Review* 87: 35–64.

———. 2014b. *Buying Time: The Delayed Crisis of Democratic Capitalism*. London: Verso.

Williams, Raymond. 1983. Capitalism. In *Keywords: A Vocabulary of Culture and Society*. Revised ed. Oxford: Oxford University Press.

Wright, Erik Olen. 2010. *Envisioning Real Utopias*. London: Verso.

Part I

Alternative Paradigms for Post-Capitalist Futures

2

The Race to Replace a Dying Neoliberalism

Walden Bello

In response to the cataclysm occasioned by the novel coronavirus, three lines of thinking have emerged. One is that the emergency necessitates extraordinary measures, but the basic structure of production and consumption is sound, and the problem lies only in determining the moment when things can return to 'normal'. One might say that this is the dominant opinion among political and business elites. Representative of this outlook is the infamous Goldman Sachs-sponsored teleconference in mid-March 2020 involving scores of stock market players, which concluded that 'there is no systemic risk. No one is even talking about that. Governments are intervening in the markets to stabilize them, and the private banking sector is well capitalized. It feels more like 9/11 than it does 2008' (Brown 2020).

A second line of thinking is that we are now in the 'new normal', and while the global economic system is not significantly out of kilter, important changes must be made to some of its elements, such as redesigning the workplace to accommodate the need for social distancing,

---

W. Bello (✉)
State University of New York, Binghamton, NY, USA

strengthening public health systems (something even Boris Johnson now advocates after Britain's National Health System saved his life), and even moving towards a Universal Basic Income.

A third response is that the pandemic provides an opportunity for transforming a system that is ridden with deep economic and political inequalities and is profoundly destabilising ecologically. One must not simply talk about accommodating a 'new normal' or expanding social safety nets, but of decisively moving toward a qualitatively new economic system.

In the global North, the needed transformation is often articulated in the form of demands for a Green New Deal marked not just by 'greening' the economy but by a significant socialisation of production and investment, democratisation of economic decision making, and radical reductions in income inequality.

In the global South, proposed strategies, while addressing the climate crisis, stress the opportunity offered by the pandemic to tackle deep-seated economic, social, and political inequalities. An eloquent example is the 'Socialist Manifesto for a Post-Covid 19 Philippines' by the *Laban ng Masa* people's coalition, a detailed list of short- and long-term initiatives, the introduction to which proclaims:

> The manner and disorder of these hegemonic players' responses to the crisis proves beyond a shadow of doubt that the old order can no longer be restored and its ruling classes can no longer administer society in the old way. The chaos, uncertainties, and fears resulting from Covid-19, depressing and dreary though they may be, are also pregnant with opportunities and challenges to develop and offer to the public a new way of organizing and managing society and its attendant political, economic, and social components. As the socialist Albert Einstein pointed out: 'We cannot solve our problems with the same thinking we used when we created them.' (Laban ng Masa 2020)

This Time Really Is Different

The first two perspectives downplay the possibilities for radical change, with some predicting that the popular response will be much like that during the 2008 financial crisis—that is, people feeling dislocated but with no appetite for much change, much less radical change. This view rests on mistakenly equating where people were during the two crises.

Crises do not always result in significant change. It is the interaction or synergy between two elements: an objective one, meaning a systemic crisis, and a subjective one, that is, the people's psychological response to it that is decisive. The global financial crisis of 2008 was a profound crisis of capitalism, but the subjective element—popular alienation from the system—had not yet reached a critical mass. Owing to the boom created by debt-financed consumer spending over two decades, people were shocked by the crisis, but they were not that alienated from the system during the crisis and its immediate aftermath.

Things are different today. The level of discontent with and alienation from neoliberalism was already very high in the global North before the coronavirus hit, owing to the established elites' inability to reverse the decline in living standards and skyrocketing inequality in the dreary decade that followed the financial crisis. In the US, the period was summed up in the popular mind as one where the elites prioritised saving the big banks over saving millions of bankrupt homeowners and ending large-scale unemployment, while in much of Europe, especially in the south, the people's experience of the last decade was captured in one word: austerity.

And in much of the global South, the chronic crisis of underdevelopment under peripheral capitalism, exacerbated by neoliberal 'reforms' since the 1980s, had already shredded the legitimacy of key institutions of globalisation like the World Bank, International Monetary Fund, and World Trade Organization, even before the 2008 crisis.

The coronavirus pandemic of 2020, in short, roared through an already destabilised global economic system suffering from a deep crisis of legitimacy. The sense that things had run out of control—certainly out of the control of the traditional political and economic managers—was the first shocking realisation. This mass perception of astonishing elite incompetence is now connecting to the already deep-seated feelings of resentment and anger boiling over from the post-financial crisis period.

So the subjective element, the psychological critical mass, is there. It is a whirlwind that is waiting to be captured by contending political forces. The question is who will succeed in harnessing it.

The global establishment will, of course, try to bring back the 'old normal'. But there has simply been too much anger, too much resentment, too much insecurity unleashed. And there's no forcing the genie back into the bottle. Though for the most part falling short of expectations, the massive fiscal and monetary interventions of capitalist states have underlined to people what is possible under another system with different priorities and values.

Neoliberalism is dying; it's only a question of whether its passing will be swift or 'slow', as Dani Rodrik (2020) characterises it.

Who Will Ride the Tiger?

Only the left and the right are serious contenders in this race to bring about another system.

Progressives have come up with a number of exciting ideas and paradigms developed over the last few decades for how to move towards a truly systemic transformation, and these go beyond the left-wing technocratic Keynesianism identified with Joseph Stiglitz and Paul Krugman. Among these truly radical alternatives are the already mentioned Green New Deal, democratic socialism, degrowth, deglobalisation, ecofeminism, food sovereignty, and the social philosophy 'Buen Vivir' (living well).

The problem is these strategies have not yet been translated into a critical mass on the ground. The usual explanation for this is that people are 'not ready for them'. But probably more significant as an explanation is that most people still associate these dynamic streams of the left with the centre left. On the ground, where it matters, the masses cannot yet distinguish these strategies and their advocates from the social democrats in Europe and the Democratic Party in the US that were implicated in the discredited neoliberal system to which they had sought to provide a 'progressive' face. For large numbers of citizens, the face of the left is still the Social Democratic Party (SPD) in Germany, the Socialist Party in France, and the Democratic Party in the US, and their records are hardly inspiring, to say the least.

In the global South, leadership of or participation in liberal democratic governments also led to left-wing parties being discredited when these coalitions adopted neoliberal measures that came under the rubric of 'structural adjustment', even as the 'Pink Tide' in Latin America ran into its own contradictions, and communist states in East Asia became state capitalist systems with a strong dose of neoliberalism. Once seen as a break with the past, the *Concertación* in Chile, the Workers' Party in Brazil, *Chavismo* in Venezuela, and the so-called Beijing Consensus are now seen as part of that past.

In short, the centre-left's thorough-going compromise with neoliberalism in the North along with progressive parties and states going along with, if not actively adopting, neoliberal measures in the South tarnished the progressive spectrum as a whole—even though it was from the non-mainstream, non-state left that the critique of neoliberalism and globalisation initially issued in the 1990s and 2000s.

It is this dubious legacy that must be decisively pushed aside if progressives are to connect with the mass anger and *ressentiment* that are now boiling over and transform them into a positive, liberating force.

Advantage: Far Right

Unfortunately, it is the extreme right that is currently best positioned to take advantage of the global discontent, because even before the pandemic, extreme right parties were already opportunistically cherry-picking elements of the anti-neoliberal stands and programmes of the independent left—for instance, the critique of globalisation, the expansion of the 'welfare state', and greater state intervention in the economy—but putting them within a right-wing gestalt.

So in Europe, you had radical right parties—among them Marine Le Pen's National Front in France, the Danish People's Party, the Freedom Party in Austria, Viktor Orbán's Fidesz Party in Hungary—abandoning parts of the old neoliberal programmes advocating liberalisation and less taxation that they had supported and now proclaiming they were for the welfare state and for more protection of the economy from international engagements, but exclusively for the benefit of the people with 'right skin color', the 'right culture', the 'right ethnic stock', the 'right religion' (Bello 2019: 123–141).

Essentially, it's the old 'national socialist' class-inclusivist but racially and culturally exclusivist formula, whose consummate practitioner in recent times has been Donald Trump. But, unfortunately, it often works in our troubled times, as shown by the unexpected string of electoral successes of the far right that have pirated large sectors of social democracy's working-class base.

Meanwhile in the global South, leaders with cross-class appeal, like Rodrigo Duterte in the Philippines and Narendra Modi in India, harnessed for their authoritarian projects the popular discontent with longtime liberal democratic regimes whose severely unequal social structures belied their democratic pretensions. This sidelined progressive parties that had either compromised with neoliberalism, were imprisoned in classist paradigms that failed to understand the new 'populist' realities, or were debilitated by sectarian feuds.

The cases of Duterte and Modi underline two phenomena associated with the rise of the far right globally. One is the importance of charismatic leadership. The great German sociologist Max Weber explored different types of authority: rational legal, traditional, and charismatic authority (Weber 1958: 245–264). Extending Weber's insights to the liberal democracies of India and the Philippines, one might say that charismatic leadership emerges to address the deep tension between the rational-legal ideological order of democratic equality that coexists with the reality of a traditional order marked by hierarchy and inequality.

The other, related insight derived from the cases of Duterte and Modi is the way charismatic leaders are able to overcome drawbacks like their regimes' poor economic performance and secure massive approval in democratic electoral exercises, then use this democratic approval to advance their authoritarian agenda. This is the democratic dialectic that lies at the heart of the new authoritarianism, whereby charismatic leaders are able to secure the massive support of ordinary citizens who may not approve of all their initiatives but are willing to give these personalities the benefit of the doubt. This dialectic between democracy and authoritarianism results in a paradox whereby the more spontaneous and free an election, the more legitimacy it provides the leader's project to move towards a full-fledged authoritarian regime (Bello 2020).

…But Don't Count Out the Left

The challenge to the left is to go beyond imagining post-capitalist regimes to materialising such alternatives in concrete social and political movements that can contend for political power. There is an urgency to this since, despite its reliance on democratic means to come to power, the right is likely to shut off political competition once in power as well as engage in a reconstruction of civil society to secure mass loyalty for authoritarian rule. It is sobering to remember that Hitler remained extremely popular among Germans even in the midst of the heaviest aerial bombardment in history, and that Franco's dictatorship in Spain and that of Salazar in neighbouring Portugal lasted almost 40 years.

But it would be foolish to count out the left. History has a complex dialectical movement, and there are often unexpected developments that open up opportunities for those bold enough to seize them, think outside the box, and willing to ride the tiger on its unpredictable route to power—of which there are many on our side, especially among the younger generation.

Two of the challenges a new left must wrestle with have been indirectly touched on here. One is that substantive reason, which has always been the strength of the left, is under circumstances such as that which prevail today of limited value when it comes to the realities of winning the political power to restructure society. The second is the role of 'affective politics', which the left has always been suspicious of, often rightfully so. There is, however, a point where a critical stance becomes rigidity. These are the two related challenges that the right has responded to successfully in the shape of charismatic leaders. To put it bluntly, does the left have to compromise with its longstanding belief in the rational voter or rational citizen and explore what it can learn from the right in this area, much like the right learned from and appropriated the left's critique of neoliberal globalisation?

But perhaps, in the short term, the lesson the left must learn is that history is unforgiving, and it rarely tolerates making the same mistake twice. Should progressives again allow discredited social democrats in Europe and Obama- and Biden-type Democrats in the US to drag progressive politics back to a new compromise with a dying neoliberalism, the consequences could be truly fatal.

If that happens, then that chilling scene in the movie *Cabaret*, where ordinary people led by a young Nazi sing 'Tomorrow Belongs to Me', has a great chance of becoming reality… again.

References

Bello, Walden. 2019. *Counterrevolution: The Global Rise of the Far Right*. Nova Scotia: Fernwood.

———. 2020. A Dangerous Liaison? Harnessing Weber to Illuminate the Relationship of Democracy and Charisma in the Philippines and India. *International Sociology* 35 (6): 691–709.

Brown, Abram. 2020. The Private Goldman Sachs Coronavirus Meeting That's Setting the Internet on Fire. *Forbes*. 16 March 2020. Accessed 10 December 2020. https://www.forbes.com/sites/abrambrown/2020/03/16/the-private-goldman-sachs-coronavirus-meeting-thats-setting-the-internet-on-fire/#ee006a450dd5

Laban ng Masa. 2020. Program: A Socialist Manifesto for a Post-Covid-19 Philippines. *Europe Solidaire Sans Frontières*, 22 April 2020. Accessed 10 December 2020. http://www.europe-solidaire.org/spip.php?article53449

Rodrik, Dani. 2020. Will Covid-19 Remake the World?. *Project Syndicate*. 6 April 2020. Accessed 10 December 2020. https://www.project-syndicate.org/commentary/will-covid19-remake-the-world-by-dani-rodrik-2020-04?barrier=accesspaylog

Weber, Max. 1958. *From Max Weber: Essays in Sociology*. Edited by Hans Gerth and C. Wright Mills. New York: Oxford University Press.

3

Ecosocialism from a Post-Development Perspective

Anitra Nelson

A striking characteristic of post-capitalist imaginaries of the twenty-first century is the extent to which they are evolving from a community of leftist movements and a movement of leftist communities. One cannot talk about, or be active in, Extinction Rebellion, degrowth, Occupy, ecofeminism, or ecosocialism without simultaneously endorsing key elements of other currents—currents that amalgamate around values and strategies that strengthen and realise environmental justice, the systemic diminution of a variety of inequities and exclusions, direct governance, and self-provisioning from food gardens to maker labs.

It seems as if the long-fragmented left is sloughing the skins of its limited and subordinate existence within various types of capitalism and latently reaching a holistic consciousness and consensus. We witness an inclusive sense of humanity amalgamating with a deep sense that we are beings not only of, but also for, an ecological universe. Such 'pluriversity'

A. Nelson (✉)
Melbourne Sustainable Society Institute, University of Melbourne, Parkville, VIC, Australia
e-mail: anitra.nelson@unimelb.edu.au

refers to saving, respecting, and co-constructing diversity within a global world without loss of solidarity and engagement, and by balancing universal rights and risks of western cultural colonisation. Beyond class struggles, globally connected capitalist economies appear like monster parasites choking their host, planet Earth. Given the environmental ravages of capitalism, we find ourselves like doctors attending our own, potentially fatal, demise. None of us can talk about a future that is not redemptive in terms of our position to Earth. In this cause we shuttle between the equally necessary, if superficially contradictory, tasks of restoration and midwifery. The 'transition' we are living is both a breakdown and a breakthrough.

This chapter considers an embroidery of activities that inform ecosocialism as a current that is determinedly humanist and ecological within this lively milieu creating and propagating post-capitalist imaginaries. Becoming visible in the 1980s, ecosocialism is, in and of itself, a community of movements and movement of communities. The *Routledge Handbook on Ecosocialism* (2021) outlines the strong influence, indeed inspiration, of strains such as women's independence and Indigenous people's movements, municipalism and anarchism, movements for food and land sovereignty, and a plethora of different subspecies of 'watermelon left'—green on the outside, red on the inside—that are both ecologically concerned and bear humanist values.

The chapter analyses two prominent tensions within ecosocialism which, in its broadest understanding, marries the ecological with socialist thought and practice. First, there are conflicts between, on the one hand, those who seek to realise ecosocialism through 'top down' democratic political parties with hierarchical national plans and policies and, on the other hand, the determinedly grassroots activism of other advocates and adherents working 'from below'. Second, there are tensions between those seeking to embed ecosocialism within recognisable forms of economies and economics—say, using alternative currencies and cooperative forms of enterprise—while others envision post-capitalism as a necessarily wholly new canvas of possibilities within which collective sufficiency, collaborative self-provisioning, and other forms of mutualism flourish without any semblance of money or market. The latter break with, or transition beyond, relationships characteristic of capitalism—workers and capitalists, workplaces and markets—whereas the former simply reform such relations of political and economic reproduction. The latter forms of ecosocialism are closer to post-development, 'worldviews and practices relating to the collective search for an ecologically wise and socially just world' (Demaria and Kothari 2017: 2595) beyond the capitalist development model.

Post-Development

In the context of post-capitalist futures, post-development offers a more constructive lens to introduce ecosocialism than positioning it within other socialist or other environmental currents. Post-development is a perspective driven by a critique of contemporary versions and practices of 'development'—only the most recent expression of a litany of criticisms of capitalism's civilising mission, recently conceptualised as 'sustainable development' as in the United Nations' Sustainable Development Goals. Ecosocialists draw on and re-interpret works of Karl Marx, who remains a prominent reference point in analyses of capitalism and, in turn, of development and post-development theory.

In the latter half of the twentieth century, certain critics of development highlighted the active underdevelopment of colonised regions. Overwhelmed by capitalist ideology, victims of unfair terms of trade and beguiling aid and credit trapped what is currently termed the Majority World under the control of the Minority World. The terms 99% and 1% reverberate. In short, post-development reveals that sustainable development is but the most recent iteration of the capitalist drive to control Earth and its people through a system of 'economy'.

Post-development, which emerged around the same time as ecosocialism, has evolved paradigms of post-growth, post-patriarchal, and post-capitalist futures, co-constructing a praxis 'in which development would no longer be the central organising principle of social life' (Demaria and Kothari 2017: 2589). Here concepts of degrowth, security of basic needs for all, horizontal governance, and social solidarity are key. In a sense, post-development is a cluster, even grab-bag, of potential alternatives and the movement is a loose network. Post-development is rich with Majority

World movements with pre-capitalist visions of a meaningful life and livelihood. Barkin and Lemus (2016: 570–571) point out that *sumak kawsay* (South America), *ubuntu* (South Africa) and *swaraj* (India) 'share five basic principles of autonomy, solidarity, self-sufficiency, productive diversification, and sustainable management of regional ecosystems'.

Ecosocialist strains engage in dialogue within and without, building on Marxian and eco-feminist critiques of capitalism, drawing on and collaborating with post-development currents. Ecosocialist theory and practice has been characterised by an increasingly weakening or nuanced Western socialist tradition and political economy discourse. Its original exposition has been prone to modifying, humanising, and greening state governance and market management to ecosocialist ends. Meanwhile, more post-development-inclined ecosocialist undercurrents have post-capitalist imaginaries that are irrevocably grounded in a grassroots, horizontalist, decentralised politics of direct and glocal democracy. ('Glocal' means the application of universal, global, principles locally.) In this latter version of post-capitalism, both the state and economy, as such, tend to evaporate.

The State in Devolution

Naomi Klein's 2014 work *This Changes Everything: Capitalism vs. the Climate* highlighted the radical repercussions of global heating. Certainly the rise of an ecological consciousness in the latter quarter of the twenty-first century changed socialism as we knew it. Breaks with a century of socialist and communist political activity and economic thought before the 1980s focused on a swing away from a productivist and workerist agenda towards broader ideas of activism and agency. Faced with growing environmental crises, an awareness of Earth's limits and rampant consumerism within advanced capitalism, ecosocialists embraced key arguments for deconstructing concepts and practices of work promulgated by the likes of André Gorz, the interrogation of the implications of technology demanded by thinkers such as Ivan Illich, and ecofeminist challenges not only to conceptions of gender and nature but also to theories and practices of reproduction.

This opening of socialist discourse was hastened by anarchist and green movements filling the void of socialist activities with respect to growing planetary distress and environmental injustices. In the process, certain ecosocialists incorporated (or evolved from) anarchist tendencies, especially with respect to the inadequacies of state power, state management, and state planning. In turn, ecosocialism has been ridden with frictions between democratic, even parliamentary, ecosocialist advances and post-development ecosocialist grassroots activism at a determinedly local level of governance and market-free production and exchange. A review of formal statements illustrates these conflictual approaches and associated strategies.

'An Ecosocialist Manifesto'—released by the New York-based Joel Kovel and Michael Löwy (2001) in Paris—humbly states a *rationale* for the existence of ecosocialism and 'a line of reasoning … for overcoming' contemporary malaise in the face of eco-catastrophe. Inviting a discursive advance, they defend the banner of 'socialism' because of its anti-capitalist soul. Marx's conceptual distinction between use value and exchange value offers a theoretical diving board to reorient 'the path and the goal of socialist production in an ecological framework'. Their vision is grounded in the Marxian emancipatory paradigm emphasising the qualitative dimension to the detriment of the quantitative. In short, addressing over-production and over-consumption requires 'a valorization of use-values over exchange-values' in order to transform needs.

The 'Belem Ecosocialist Declaration' written by Canadian editor of online ecosocialist journal *Climate and Capitalism* Ian Angus along with Angus et al. (2008) has a more strident ring, starting: 'Humanity today faces a stark choice: ecosocialism or barbarism.' A cursory integration of everyone in the revolution leaves them looking somewhat like cannon fodder once the so-called 'radical transformation' is spelled out, implying state planning and explicitly state investment to control sectors such as energy, transport, manufacture, and 'sustainable agro-ecosystems'. Written for the World Socialist Forum (Brazil, January 2009), the statement perplexingly refers to 'a transformed economy founded on the non-monetary values of social justice and ecological balance' but assumes a market, even if not ruled by capital, and obscures the participatory and decision-making mechanisms of an all-embracing democracy.

Responses made within the first month of its release as a draft include a call by New York ecosocialist and editor of *Capitalism Nature Socialism* Salvatore Engel-Di Mauro ('saed') to emphasise that the full panoply of agents in this transformation control their means of production explicitly to fulfil their needs. Moreover, Belgian agriculturalist and ecosocialist activist Daniel Tanuro insists on a clearer and more decisive reduction of energy and material use (Angus et al. 2008). A first principle of degrowth is to reduce inequities. Degrowth argues for deep reductions in material and energy use but, at the same time, the satisfaction of everyone's basic needs.

It is clear in other works by Kovel and Löwy (2001) that they appreciate the need to target overconsumption and to develop decentralised direct democracy. However, Angus (2017: 161) has remained querulous about Tanuro's degrowth point, grossly misrepresenting degrowth arguments and charging that 'we are never going to build a global movement unless we recognize and accept that two-thirds of the world actually needs "more stuff"'. The interventions made by saed and Tanuro exposed a subterranean culture and political drive within the ecosocialist movement to embrace open, local, and horizontal forms of governance complementing more profound understandings of ecological crises and limits.

In the First Ecosocialist International (Participants 2017) statement on global and local strategies, such grassroots activists find their voices, appropriately with plans of action in the short, medium, and long terms. Their statement makes a quantum leap and offers the following distinguishing and representative characteristics. Its subtitle is 'Weaving Ourselves to Mother Earth'. It is written in 'the enchanted mountains of Yaracuy, where the guardian goddess of nature lives', in Venezuela in early November. Its authors are some 100 voices from five continents and 19 countries, including a dozen Indigenous peoples of Latin America and many Venezuelan ecosocialist activists. It is 'the articulation of a combined strategy and plan of action for the salvation of Mother Earth'. It anoints Indigenous peoples as 'the first and original eco-socialists'. In this statement ecosocialism 'symbolizes insurgency and love, it is spiritual, pluri-cultural and multi-ethnic, and it teaches decolonization and anti-imperialism'. They profess an ecosocialism 'based on what we do and what we are'.

This statement is post-development in its scope and prefigurative in its approach to post-capitalism. It is, as it were, 'new testament' ecosocialism: we are the being of our agency, judge us by our acts. Inasmuch as the authors embrace Earth, they are 'outward-looking' with a mission beyond human politics. As if speaking to saed, they write: 'We will not leave food sovereignty only in the hands of the state; rather we will take responsibility for it as communities'. Because here we find, in and with these peoples, the living seeds (don't call them remnants) of Uruguayan socialist Eduardo Galeano's 'community-based mode of production' (Nelson 2018).

Moreover, don't talk of stages or of providing for the needs of others: 'We', write the Participants 'take responsibility for our utopia as an eternal journey'. This is as much a statement of intent as a call to action—the intent of activists the world over who concur with ecosocialist values and principles. With it, the state devolves or disintegrates into localised governance:

> We will harvest the [ancestral communitarian] socialism of the 21st century and all centuries, until we arrive at a communism of the sun, wind and water, receiving all spiritualities together, towards the defense of the common, and the free integration of languages and forms of exchange, without any loss of autonomy or originality. We will be united in diversity. (Participants 2017)

The Market Disappears

The 2017 First Ecosocialist International statement refers to the decolonising anti-capitalist Venezuelan social movement in its 'visions of eliminating money and returning to the ancestral mode of production, consumption and distribution' where exchange of goods and services are based on non-market values of sharing, collective effort, and mutual support 'with solidarity and without monetary compensations'. In contrast to twentieth-century Marxian preoccupations with productivist technologies and the state, the statement strongly focuses on the primary concern of Marx with the *relations* of production. They incorporate Marx's scepticism of the state and the market. They give body to communal forms of governance and provisioning that exist today in the direct, conscious, active, and reflective rule of communities, such as Zapatista and certain other Indigenous and peasant Mexican communities (Barkin and Lemus 2016) and those influenced by Abdullah Öcalan, the Apoist strain generating Kurdish grassroots democratic autonomy (Aslan 2016).

In *Communal Luxury: The Political Imaginary of the Paris Commune*, Kristen Ross (2015) shows that these currents within, and in dialogue with, ecosocialist currents are not new. A theoretical founder of ecosocialism is the nineteenth-century artist and socialist activist William Morris, whose views are consistent with the grassroots ecosocialist tendency. Morris and his contemporary 'precursor to contemporary developments in eco-socialism', Jacques Élisée Reclus, agree that all land—from which the materials for food, shelter, and clothing are grown—as well as other forms of production of basic needs must be held as commons and subject to commoning (Ross 2015: 138, 140–141). In their work, Ross finds:

> An emphasis on the kind of regional self-sufficiency that was the watchword of the Commune. A world of smaller, regional productive units and intensive but preservationist land use, a decentralized world where small-scale industry was dispersed and combined with agriculture: this was the vision. Self-sufficiency at the regional level would diminish if not bring an end to the need for international trade. Production for a local market was desirable and rational…. (Ross 2015: 141)

What we find, then, is a vastly different imaginary and implicitly distinctive transformational route from the top-down vision of an ecosocialist society found at the System Change Not Climate Change Ecosocialist Coalition website, which refers to planning and public transit, shortening the working week, and increasing production in the renewable energy sector.

In the Theoretical Moorings section of the *Routledge Handbook on Ecosocialism* is a chapter on money-free economies. This non-monetary line evolves from the conclusion that, inasmuch as communities directly decide on their basic needs and how to fulfil them locally, there is no need for a market at all. Collective sufficiency means production on and for a pre-existing demand. The producers know where the product needs to go, who it is for. It is simply a logistical matter of distribution from the point of production to the intended consumer, user, or recipient of services. Thus, given that communities are fully governing, their resources are commons, and they share their product on the basis of need, there is no place for money, market, or even economics as we know it (Nelson 2021).

We find, then, that this grassroots and post-development vision and strategy for transformation cannot be easily combined with, but rather collides with, the more visible, let's say 'Minority World approach', within ecosocialism. We live at a critical juncture where environmentalists and leftists more generally have failed to resist or reverse the worst onslaughts of the capitalist system in which they are compelled to live. The ravages of capitalism now amount to massive planetary failures that are making other species extinct and threatening the future of human life itself. Thus there is an urgency to decide to act in one direction. This does not mean under one leadership or authority, but it does mean agreeing on certain universal principles and structures while allowing their pluriverse application.

Conclusion

As capitalist practices are increasingly and more generally understood as incapable of fulfilling the basic needs of everyone and the planet, certain ecosocialist and associated post-development currents show that there are feasible, indeed preferable, community-based ways of living beyond capitalism. These post-capitalist tendencies share universal, humane, and ecological values applied glocally in creative and multi-various forms. They approach Earth as a commons and rely on sophisticated forms of local governance with global networks structuring planetary relations. These post-capitalist ways of living pursue prefigurative embodiments that are pluriverse, open, and dynamic. Are they 'alternatives' or the main game?

References

Angus, Ian. 2017. *A Redder Shade of Green: Intersections of Science and Socialism*. New York: Monthly Review Press.

Angus, Ian, Joel Kovel, and Michael Löwy. 2008. Belem Ecosocialist Declaration. Accessed April 20, 2020. https://climateandcapitalism.com/2008/12/16/belem-ecosocialist-declaration-a-call-for-signatures/.

Aslan, Azize (trans.). 2016. Economic Self-Governance in Democratic Autonomy: The Example of Bakur (Turkish Kurdistan). Co-operation in Mesopotamia website. Accessed April 20, 2020. https://mesopotamia.coop/economic-self-governance-in-democratic-autonomy-the-example-of-bakur/.

Barkin, David, and Blanca Lemus. 2016. Third World Alternatives for Building Post-capitalist Worlds. *Review of Radical Political Economics* 48 (4): 569–576.

Brownhill, Leigh, Salvatore Engel-Di Mauro, Terran Giacomini, Ana Isla, Michael Löwy, and Terisa Turner, eds. 2021. *The Routledge Handbook on Ecosocialism*. New York: Routledge.

Demaria, Federico, and Ashish Kothari. 2017. The Post-development Dictionary Agenda: Paths to the Pluriverse' (Special issue: The Development Dictionary @25: Post-Development and its Consequences, guest ed. Aram Ziai). *Third World Quarterly* 38 (12): 2588–2599.

Klein, Naomi. 2014. *This Changes Everything: Capitalism vs the Climate*. London: Allen Lane.

Kovel, Joel, and Michael Löwy. 2001. An Ecosocialist Manifesto. *Ecosocialist Horizons* website. Accessed April 20, 2020. http://ecosocialisthorizons.com/2001/09/an-ecosocialist-manifesto/.

Nelson, Anitra. 2018. The Political Economy of Space and Time in Eduardo Galeano. *Progress in Political Economy*. Accessed April 20, 2020. http://ppesydney.net/political-economy-space-time-eduardo-galeano/.

———. 2021. Moneyfree Economies and Ecosocialism. In *The Routledge Handbook on Ecosocialism*, eds. Leigh Brownhill, Salvatore Engel-Di Mauro, Terran Giacomini, Ana Isla, Michael Löwy, and Terisa Turner. New York: Routledge.

Participants. 2017. *Combined Strategy and Plan of Action of the First Ecosocialist International*. 31 October–3 November, Cumbe of Veroes, Bolivarian Republic of Venezuela. Ecosocialist Horizons website. Accessed April 20, 2020. http://ecosocialisthorizons.com/wp-content/uploads/2017/12/Combined-Strategy-and-Plan-of-Action-of-the-First-Ecosocialist-International.pdf.

Ross, Kristin. 2015. *Communal Luxury: The Political Imaginary of the Paris Commune*. London/Brooklyn: Verso.

4

Post-Capitalism Now: A Community Economies Approach

Jenny Cameron

Post-Capitalism Is Already Here

Post-capitalism is most commonly understood in temporal terms as a new political economic stage that will follow capitalism. Great hope is attached to the idea that capitalism will inevitably unravel, and that in the current period this might be triggered by the seriousness of the environmental emergency and gathering socio-economic tensions. There is, however, a different understanding of 'capitalism'. What if capitalism is understood as a way of framing the world, and what if this framing is understood as having powerful effects that include normalising one vision of economy and establishing one set of options for political action? The understanding that capitalism is one way of framing the economy is the starting point for a community economies approach to capitalism—with implications for how post-capitalism is understood.

J. Cameron (✉)
University of Newcastle, Callaghan, NSW, Australia
e-mail: Jenny.Cameron@newcastle.edu.au

Community economies is associated with the work of J.K. Gibson-Graham and her two major works, *The End of Capitalism (As We Knew It): A Feminist Critique of Political Economy* (1996) and *A Postcapitalist Politics* (2006). In community economies scholarship and activism, the idea of capitalocentrism is pivotal. The term was coined by J.K. Gibson-Graham (1996) to describe how capitalism is widely understood not just as the dominant economic system but as the ultimate determinant of so much that goes on in the world. The effect of a capitalocentric framing of the economy is to privilege capitalist economic activity and relationships, and to demote and devalue other economic activities and relationships. Community economies scholarship and activism recognises that there is a diversity of economic activities and relationships that are not capitalist and that are not necessarily subsumed to capitalist dynamics. This economic diversity that exists across the globe, including in so-called capitalist economies, is valued because it is what we have 'at hand' to nurture economies that are more socially, economically, and environmentally just. In this way of thinking, post-capitalism is already here but only dimly visible when capitalism is given centre stage and accorded the central role.

Community economies scholarship and activism contributes to strengthening the post-capitalist world that is already here through two overarching strategies: first, by making existing economic diversity more visible; second, by working with others to help strengthen the existing economic activities and relationships that are already enacting the type of post-capitalist world that so many of us yearn for. This chapter discusses these two strategies, and it uses examples from a range of urban contexts to illustrate how these strategies are being put into practice by community economies scholars and activists.

Making Economic Diversity More Visible

One of the tools used in the community economies field to communicate economic diversity is the image of the economy as an iceberg (see Fig. 4.1). The small portion of the iceberg that sits above the waterline represents those economic activities that are associated with capitalism:

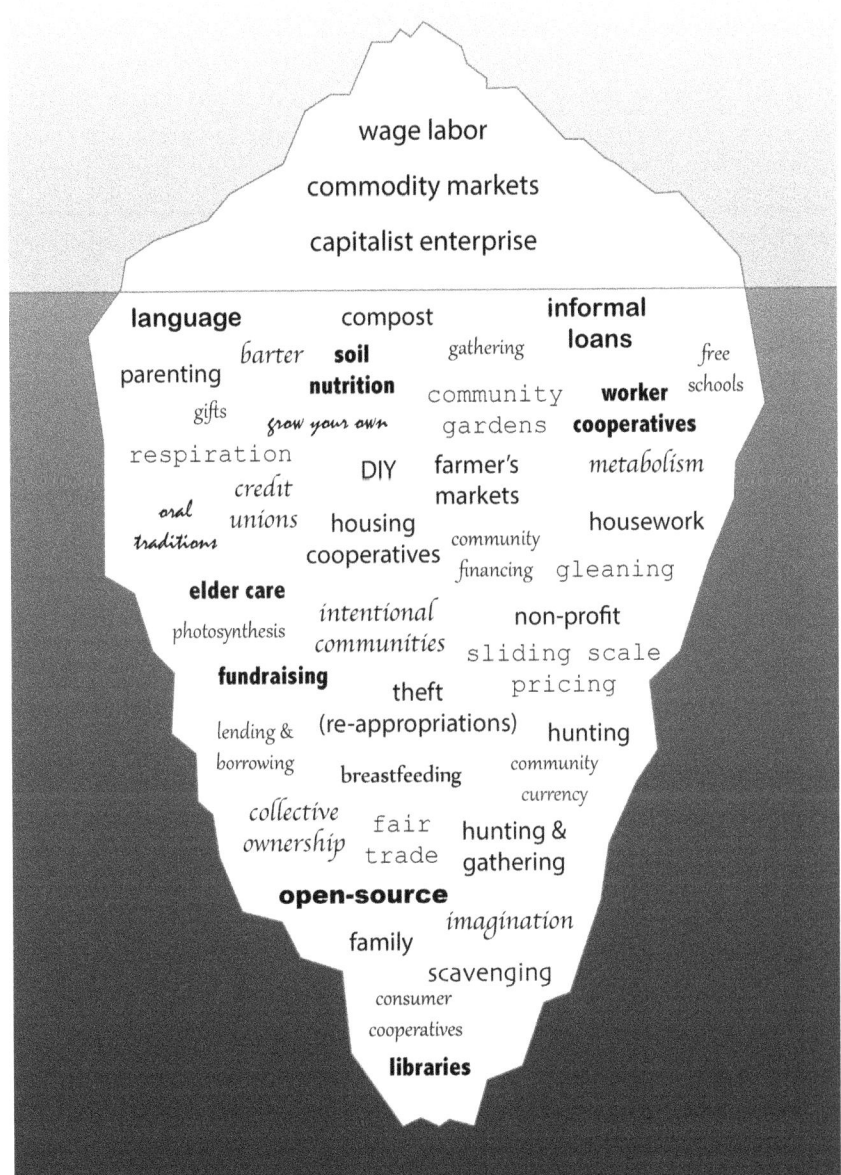

Fig. 4.1 The Diverse Economies Iceberg. (Source: Diverse Economies Iceberg by Community Economies Collective is licensed under a Creative Commons Attribution-ShareAlike 4.0 International License. Available from https://www.communityeconomies.org/resources/diverse-economies-iceberg)

workers employed in capitalist enterprises and being paid a wage to produce goods and services that are sold through commodity markets. Below the waterline is a diverse array of economic activities and relationships, some of which are easy to recognise as being economic in nature (such as fair trade and bartering) and some of which seem to be less obviously economic (such as photosynthesis and composting) but which nevertheless provide the ecological 'work' on which societies rely. The iceberg image is one counter to capitalocentric thinking that privileges capitalism as the dominant economic form and driver, and casts into shadow the diversity of other economic activities and relationships which are prevalent across the globe, which have their own dynamics, and which are already being used (or have the potential to be used) to enact a post-capitalist world now.

Building on the iceberg image, community economies researchers and activists have developed a systematic means of reframing the economy by considering the diversity of five economic dimensions:

- The forms of *labour* that are used to secure what people need to survive. This includes paid labour, but also unpaid labour, such as housework, and labour that is paid in other ways, such as reciprocal labour.
- The types of *enterprises* through which such surplus value is produced and distributed. This includes capitalist enterprises, but also other types of capitalist enterprises, such as social enterprises (which like capitalist firms have an owner/worker structure but are based on motivations other than profit maximisation), and non-capitalist enterprises, such as worker-owned cooperatives.
- The means of *transacting* goods and services. This includes monetary-based market transactions, but also non-market transactions, such as household flows and gift-giving, and the transactions that take place through non-monetary-based markets, such as local trading systems.
- The forms of *property* through which resources are managed (or mismanaged). This includes private property, but also open-access property, such as the atmosphere and open-source software, and collectively 'owned' property, such as Indigenous land and state-managed assets.

- The types of *finance* used to support economic and other activities. This includes market-based finance, but also non-market-based finance, such as sweat equity, family financing, and rotating savings and credit associations, and other types of financial markets such as state-based lending.

The recently published *Handbook of Diverse Economies* (Gibson-Graham and Dombroski 2020) is based around these five economic dimensions and includes framing essays that overview each dimension and chapters that investigate specific economic activities and relationships that fall within each dimension.

This work on economic diversity sheds light on the array of economic activities and relationships that are present across the globe; and it helps direct attention to those existing activities and relationships that are already enacting the type of post-capitalist world that is too-often consigned to the future, and to those activities and relationships that might be used to build post-capitalist worlds now.

The way in which recognising economic diversity might contribute to building post-capitalist worlds is demonstrated by recent studies conducted by members of the Community Economies Research Network in very different urban contexts. One study by Christian Anderson (2020) was based on three years of ethnographic research in the far West Side of Midtown Manhattan in New York City, an area known as Clinton/Hell's Kitchen. This neighbourhood can easily be understood through a capitalocentric framing with the processes of gentrification and displacement that the neighbourhood is experiencing explained in terms of dynamics of capitalist accumulation and capitalist value making, dynamics which are 'played out' through real estate speculation and which are transforming this previously run-down neighbourhood.

However, one of Anderson's key informants, a resident and tenant organiser in the neighbourhood since the late 1970s, encouraged Anderson to consider other framings. Bob explained to Anderson that he was not that interested in an analysis that focused on structural forces and which emphasised how powerful those forces are. Although he agreed with the basis for this analysis, for Bob it was not that useful as it did not offer him 'traction to think differently or to undertake different forms of practical action in his own situation and struggles' (2020: xv). Bob's explanation for why he is interested in a different type of analysis parallels Gibson-Graham's explanation for why she came up with the term capitalocentrism. In a recent podcast interview, Gibson (2020) reflects on how scholarship and activism that seek to understand capitalism in order to bring about economic change too often quash possibilities for change by reproducing over again a narrative of capitalism as a dominant force with a seemingly never-ending capacity to adapt and conquer. Like Bob, Gibson-Graham is interested in understandings that might 'open up' rather than 'close down' avenues for economic and political action and change.

To 'open up' options, Anderson drew on a diverse economy framing of the Clinton/Hell's Kitchen neighbourhood and attended to the everyday and seemingly mundane economic and political activities of those who live and work in the area. One thing that stood out from the research was the strength of people's collective endeavours to shape the neighbourhood and secure livelihoods in a context in which paid work was becoming increasingly precarious. It is here in the collective endeavours of those who live and work in the area that Anderson sees the potential for transformation, as he writes: 'the people of the neighbourhood as a whole have more collective social power and social wealth among themselves than ever before' (2020: 214). For a tenant organiser such as Bob, this research points to the value of economic and political activism that is directed towards supporting and fostering cooperation. In terms of post-capitalism, this research points to the possibilities for economic and political collectivity that already exist in a neighbourhood such as Clinton/Hell's Kitchen and that might be strengthened (potentially by tenant organisers such as Bob).

Other studies in this part of the world draw similar conclusions. Lauren Hudson's research on the solidarity economy in New York City finds that the food cooperatives, community land trusts, credit unions, mutual aid organisations, community gardens, and housing cooperatives that form part of this economy are based on values of social justice, ecological sustainability, cooperation, mutualism, and democracy (see Cameron 2020). Hudson notes that much of the work of creating and sustaining economic possibilities in the city is being carried out by black women and that the work is a material necessity to secure what is needed for survival but also a political commitment to live in the world in solidarity with others. For Hudson, this research is a means of showing 'how things that are usually managed privately within the household can be managed in cooperation and … how there is a viable alternative to individualised ways of living in the city' (cited in Cameron 2020).

In the very different context of the Kalyanpur slum in Dhaka, Bangladesh, Waliuzzaman (2020) also highlights how economic diversity is the basis for economic and political activism. Slums have long been seen as a product of capitalist economic development starting with Engels' depiction of the slums of Manchester in the 1840s and the horrors of industrial capitalism. Waliuzzaman is equally concerned with addressing living conditions in the Kalyanpur slum but, like Anderson and Hudson, he starts with the diversity of existing economic activities and relationships in this urban locale. He finds that slum dwellers are contributing their time, effort, and creativity to protect their families' livelihoods and maintain the liveability of the slum through initiatives such as forming small cooperatives that help to secure financial security, establishing a community-based waste collection system (to which households pay a small monthly fee which is used to employ five slum dwellers to run the system), and voluntarily managing and maintaining the shared toilets and tube wells.

Waliuzzaman argues that the slum dwellers are creating an urban commons 'not out of the desire of the people to be revolutionary or to protest against the hegemony of global capitalism but out of the common urge of earning a living and securing a place to live. In that process, they collaborate, help, care, negotiate, avoid, and sometimes are in conflict with others' (2020: 191). The economic work of creating and maintaining this urban commons is intertwined with political activism, including resisting evictions and protesting the actions of local MPs in order to take a stand against land grabbing by the state and political elites.

These studies that shed light on existing economic diversity in urban contexts highlight how economic diversity is associated with efforts to build urban economies that are based on values such as cooperation and collectivity. In so doing, those who live and work in these places are contributing to the project of building post-capitalist worlds now. Identifying economic diversity and the ways it is being used for more just and sustainable economies is one strategy used by community economies scholars and activists. A second is to engage in actions that might strengthen these existing economic activities and relationships.

Strengthening Post-Capitalist Worlds

One of the characteristics of community economies scholarship and activism is that there is no predetermined blueprint or recipe for how to proceed with strengthening post-capitalist worlds. Instead, community economies scholars and activists are interested in the multitude of ways that diverse economic activities and relationships might be harnessed to build more ethical economies. This means moving from the inventorying of the five economic dimensions (above) to considering the ethical potential of these dimensions, as follows:

- How might diverse forms of *labour* be used to help us to survive well, especially when we take into account not just our own wellbeing, but the wellbeing of other people and the planet?
- How do different types of *enterprises* produce and distribute surplus in ways that contribute to the social and environmental health of the world around?
- How are *transactions* of goods and services occurring so that relationships between people and environments are being nourished, including those in distant places that provide vital inputs to meet others' needs?
- How are different forms of *property* being used to maintain, restore, and replenish the gifts of nature and intellect that all humans rely on?
- How is *finance* being used to store and use our surplus and savings so that people and the planet are supported and sustained?

The shift from inventorying economic diversity to considering how economic diversity is already being used or might be used to build more ethical economies is explored in the 2013 publication *Take Back the Economy: An Ethical Guide for Transforming our Communities* (Gibson-Graham et al. 2013). This book features actions that include direct action

4 Post-Capitalism Now: A Community Economies Approach

by groups of people to develop ethical economic initiatives and policy development that will provide support for these initiatives. What follows is just a glimpse into how community economies scholars and activists are engaged in direct and policy action in various urban contexts.

A current direct action by members of the Community Economies Research Network is The Interdependence, which was launched in November 2020 as an alliance that includes enterprises that produce and distribute surplus in ways that acknowledge how people and the planet's survival are interdependent and reliant on practices of mutual care (see https://www.communityeconomies.org/interdependence). Enterprises that sign up to the alliance use *idt.* as a signifier to replace and displace more familiar enterprise signifiers such as Inc. and Ltd that are associated with corporate norms based on the values of competition and profit maximisation. One of the first enterprises to sign up was Company Drinks idt., a social enterprise based in Barking and Dagenham in the east of London that was registered in 2015 as a Community Interest Company (see http://companydrinks.info/about/). Company Drinks idt. runs a range of initiatives and takes its name from its contemporary re-creation of 'picking days', a practice from the early 1800s to the 1950s when up to 250,000 working-class Londoners (mainly women and children) would leave the East End in late summer to spend weeks in the Kent countryside picking hops and fruits. On one level Company Drinks idt. engages in a cooperative practice of hops and fruit harvesting, beverage production, and drinks trading, while on another it continues to make the urban and rural connection explicit, and links an older working class culture with the diverse cultures of recently arrived immigrants to this part of the city.

Although it is in its early days, The Interdependence aims to be a worldwide alliance, and to include initiatives such as those discussed above in places as far afield as New York and Dhaka. This effort is an important illustration of how community economies scholars and activists tackle the issue of 'scale'. As opposed to the strategy of 'scaling up' from something small to something large, community economies scholars and activists subscribe to a combined strategy of showing how post-capitalist economies are already ubiquitous, strengthening what is already here through connecting initiatives, and thereby helping to proliferate what we already have.

A recent policy initiative by members of the Community Economies Research Network involves using new tools of measurement to help value, in policy terms, the economic diversity that is usually invisible and uncounted (including voluntary unpaid labour, environmental care services, everyday ecological practices, and wellbeing improvements). Drawing on the Community Economy Return on Investment (introduced in *Take Back the Economy*), a group of 'community economies accountants' have applied the tool to R-Urban, an urban commons initiative started in 2011 by the activist architecture practice Atelier d'Architecture Autogérée (aaa) in Colombes, a multicultural municipality on the suburban outskirts of Paris where residents have incomes below the national average and where social housing towers are interspersed with single family dwellings (Petrescu et al. 2020). Projects run through R-Urban include a micro-farm, family garden plots, teaching space, compost school, and a self-constructed community recycling and eco-construction centre that include workshop space, materials storage, and a design studio and apartment. According to the calculations, the initial Community Economy Investment of €1.2million resulted in an annual Community Economy Return on Investment of 180 per cent. Such demonstration of the obvious benefit of R-Urban was not enough to convince a newly elected right-wing municipal council to change their plans to concrete over the urban commons and turn it into a car park. Nevertheless, this community economies accounting exercise has helped the model to be replicated in three additional urban areas of Paris (in Gennevilliers, Nanterre, and Bagneux by aaa) and in London (in Hackney Wick, and Poplar by PublicWorks) with funding support from the relevant municipalities. Community economies scholars and activists are not naïve in thinking that the world will easily be made post-capitalist and that initiatives such as R-Urban will be uncontested but they are committed to the ongoing struggle that is involved in making post-capitalist worlds now.

Conclusion

Like all those concerned with a post-capitalist future, community economies scholars and activists yearn for a world which is more just and sustainable, and in which economic practices serve rather than undermine such values. For community economies scholars and activists this world is already here. It is here in the diversity of economic activities and relationships that already exist but are rendered invisible each time the world is cast as capitalist. This world is here in the initiatives that harness economic diversity to enact economic practices that nourish the interdependencies between people and between people and environments. This means that the attention of community economies scholars and activists is turned to strategies that might help this economic diversity become more visible and to strategies that might strengthen those efforts that are, in the here and now, creating more just and more sustainable worlds.

References

Anderson, Christian. 2020. *Urbanism without Guarantees: The Everyday Life of a Gentrifying West Side Neighborhood.* Minneapolis: University of Minnesota Press.

Cameron, Jenny. 2020. The Movement Space of New York's Solidarity Economy. *CE News*, October 1. Accessed December 18, 2020. https://www.communityeconomies.org/news/movement-space-new-yorks-solidarity-economy.

Gibson, Katherine. 2020. Interview by Oshan Jarow. Musing Mind Podcast, October 10. Accessed December 18, 2020. https://musingmind.org/podcasts/katherine-gibson-postcapitalism.

Gibson-Graham, J.K. 1996. *The End of Capitalism (As We Knew It): A Feminist Critique of Political Economy.* Oxford: Blackwell.

———. 2006. *A Postcapitalist Politics.* Minneapolis: University of Minnesota Press.

Gibson-Graham, J.K., and Kelly Dombroski, eds. 2020. *The Handbook of Diverse Economies.* Cheltenham, UK: Edward Elgar.

Gibson-Graham, J.K., Jenny Cameron, and Stephen Healy. 2013. *Take Back the Economy: An Ethical Guide for Transforming our Communities.* Minneapolis: University of Minnesota Press.

Petrescu, Doina, Constantin Petcou, Maliha Safri, and Katherine Gibson. 2020. Calculating the Value of the Commons: Generating Resilient Urban Futures.

Environmental Policy and Governance. Accessed December 18, 2020. https://onlinelibrary.wiley.com/toc/17569338/0/0.

Waliuzzaman, S.M. 2020. *A Commons Perspective on Urban Informal Settlements: A Study of Kalyanpur Slum in Dhaka, Bangladesh*. PhD Thesis. Christchurch NZ: University of Canterbury.

5

Collective Sufficiency: Degrowth as a Political Project

Samuel Alexander and Brendan Gleeson

If capitalism is coming to an end in coming years or decades as it collides with various ecological and financial limits, how can we actively design the end of this mode of political economy rather than wait for its collapse? Or even, if necessary, how can we design for the collapse of capitalism in ways that make the best of a destabilised situation? Capitalism certainly isn't going to lie down like a lamb at the polite request of Left-leaning environmentalists. What this means is that sustainability and justice advocates with radical visions of post-capitalist futures need to think very carefully about the question of *strategy* and *transition*. More specifically, we must confront the question of where and how to invest time, energy, and resources, if we genuinely seek a fundamentally different type of economic system 'beyond capitalism'.[1]

---

[1] This chapter draws from and develops two previous publications: Samuel Alexander and Brendan Gleeson, *Degrowth in the Suburbs: A Radical Urban Imaginary* (2019, Palgrave) Ch 7; and Samuel Alexander, 'Post-Capitalism by Design not Disaster' *Ecological Citizen* 3(Suppl B): 13–21 (2020).

S. Alexander (✉) • B. Gleeson
Melbourne Sustainable Society Institute, University of Melbourne, Parkville, VIC, Australia
e-mail: brendan.gleeson@unimelb.edu.au

In the prehistory of the COVID-19 pandemic, we explored in our book *Degrowth in the Suburbs* (Alexander and Gleeson 2019) the prospects for a systemic transition away from capitalism via degrowth—planned, managed, or imposed. We argued degrowth is the most coherent paradigm for transcending the machinic economics of growth inherent to the existing capitalist system.

Building on that post-capitalist vision, in this chapter we explore the transitional question of how that imaginary could be driven into existence as a grounded form of political economy. In doing so we also highlight the role grassroots social movements and alternative economic experiments might need to play in prefiguring degrowth economies and creating the cultural conditions for a politics and macroeconomics of degrowth to emerge. We begin with a brief definitional statement.

What is Degrowth?

Degrowth is a movement that sees the goal of limitless economic growth as being incompatible with a finite planet. From this perspective, the notion of 'green growth'—where economies are envisioned to grow but in sustainable ways—is a dangerous but enduring myth (Hickel and Kallis 2019). Despite decades of extraordinary technological advance and deep faith in market mechanisms to bring environmental salvation, the so-called greening of capitalism has only produced ever-greater devastation. What is needed is a degrowth process of planned economic contraction that downshifts global material and energy demands to sustainable levels. The growth imperatives of capitalism, however, will not accept this, which is why sustainability implies a post-capitalist world.

Environmental sustainability, of course, cannot be isolated from social justice concerns. The growthists maintain that the only path to poverty alleviation is via the strategy of GDP growth, on the assumption that 'a rising tide will lift all boats'. Given that a degrowth economy deliberately seeks a non-growing economy—on the assumption that a rising tide will *sink* all boats—poverty alleviation must be achieved more directly, via distribution of wealth and power, both nationally and internationally. In other words (and to change the metaphor) a degrowth economy would seek to eliminate poverty and achieve distributive equity not by baking an ever-larger pie but by slicing it differently. From a global perspective, the post-development literature is an indispensable guide to what degrowth scholar Serge Latouche calls the 'decolonisation of the imaginary'.

Prerequisites for a Degrowth Transition

Recently the Danish political economist Hubert Buch-Hansen (2018) published a paper which outlined a conceptual framework that is useful for thinking about how paradigm shifts in political economy occur. He argued that there are four main prerequisites:

- First, there must be a crisis or series of crises that cannot be resolved within the existing mode of political economy;
- Second, there must be a coherent alternative political project;
- Third, there must be a comprehensive coalition of social forces attempting to produce the alternative paradigm through political struggle and social activism; and
- Finally, there must be broad-based cultural consent, even passive consent, for the new paradigm.

We're going to adopt this framework, add our own analytical flesh to its theoretical bones, and use it to discuss the question of a degrowth transition to a post-capitalist society.

Capitalism Is Not in Crisis: Capitalism *Is* the Crisis

The first prerequisite, then, for a paradigm shift in the existing mode of political economy is crisis—but not just any crisis. It must be a crisis or series of crises in the system that the system itself cannot resolve. There are many reasons to think this prerequisite is met. Growth economics is sometimes called the 'ideology of the cancer cell' and this provocative metaphor neatly summarises the fatal anomaly in capitalism, namely, that on the one hand, it *must* keep growing for stability, and, on the other hand, for various ecological and financial reasons, it simply *cannot* keep growing. Like a chorus of others, we don't believe capitalism can resolve this fundamental contradiction, which is creating conditions for a new, post-capitalist paradigm to replace it (Hickel and Kallis 2019). Accordingly, for the purpose of this forward-looking chapter, we will assume that the capitalist mode of political economy is ridden with irresolvable ecological and social crises such that, one way or another, the future will be post-capitalist.

An Alternative Political Project

The second prerequisite for a paradigm shift in political economy—for a degrowth transition, in particular—is the existence of an alternative political project. This isn't the forum to comprehensively articulate and defend this alternative political project, so we're just going to state it, or one version of it, in order to show that an alternative post-capitalist political project is beginning to take form.

The following political agenda is, in our view, both coherent and attractive, but it will soon become clear how disconnected it is from political realism in developed nations (or anywhere) today. Of course, we would argue that this is an indictment of mainstream politics, not the theory of degrowth. However, the political and social unpalatability of degrowth is a point to which we will return, because it has implications on the question of strategy. In a time of rising authoritarianism and political reaction in general, it is likely to be fiercely opposed by those clinging to the wreckage of the sinking ship. Nonetheless, nothing good will come from ill preparation for change that might come suddenly and unexpectedly. Therefore, we offer the following policy programme as an exercise in radical political imagination; a set of pivots and plot points for transition to a degrowth society:

- *Alternatives to GDP*: First, any political transition beyond capitalism requires transcending the GDP fetish and establishing better and more nuanced ways to measure societal progress, such as the Genuine Progress Indicator. Post-growth measures of progress like this open up space for political parties to implement policy and institutional changes—including those which we are about to review—which would genuinely improve social wellbeing and enhance ecological conditions, even if these would not increase, and would probably even decrease, GDP.
- *Diminishing Resource Caps*: If the rich, overgrown economies are serious about moving toward a just and sustainable human inhabitation of Earth, then first, we must acknowledge that we are hugely over-consuming our fair share of global resources, and second, we must institute diminishing resource caps which put strict limits on national resource flows. Fortunately, this would incentivise the efficient use of resources and dis-incentivise waste, and lead to degrowth in ecological impacts. Eco-socialists would argue that reducing societal material and energy flows will require significant nationalisation of key industries for stability during the planned contraction (Smith 2016), whereas eco-anarchists would argue that a confederation of small self-governing communities would be the better path (Trainer 2010). This debate is likely to continue and it may be that this controversy can only be resolved through practical experimentation, not theory.
- *Reduced Working Hours (in Formal Economy)*: One obvious implication of diminishing resource caps is that a lot less resource-intensive production and consumption would take place in a degrowth economy. This would almost certainly lead to reduced GDP. To avoid the unemployment that typically flows from declining GDP, a degrowth economy would reduce work in the formal economy and share available work amongst the working population, while also placing increased value on the 'care economy'. Financial security in a contracting economy could also be maintained through policies like a Participation Income, Universal Basic Services, or a job guarantee, as noted in the final bullet point. (We will return to the question of informal or household economies in the next section.)

- *Rethink Government Spending*: Currently, as a general statement, governments shape their policies and spend their money in order to promote economic growth. Under a degrowth paradigm, it follows that government spending would need to be fundamentally reconsidered. For example, fewer airports, roads, and tanks; more bike lanes and public transport. How governments spend money is one way to vote for what exists in the world. Rethinking government spending would also need to go hand in hand with transformations in the systemic provision of basic services. For example, Cubans have better health on average than US citizens and yet spend an estimated 90 per cent less on healthcare per capita (Hamblin 2016). This suggests that there is ample room to provide for basic services in an affordable way while also making more public money available to fund other social projects (like public housing or renewable energy systems).
- *Renewable Energy Transition*: In anticipation of the foreseeable stagnation and eventual decline of fossil fuel supplies, and recognising the grave dangers presented by climate change, a degrowth economy would divest from fossil fuels and invest in a renewable energy transition with the urgency of 'war time' mobilisation. This will be much more affordable and technically feasible if energy demand across society is greatly reduced, and that is a key feature of a degrowth society (Alexander and Floyd 2018). The energy transition needed cannot just involve 'greening' the supply of energy, it must also involve greatly reduced demand. This means anticipating and managing what Australian activist-analyst David Holmgren calls 'the energy descent future'.
- *Banking and Finance*: Our systems of banking and finance currently have a growth imperative built into their structures. Any degrowth society would have to create systems that did not require growth for stability. Debt jubilees would probably be required, especially with respect to the poorest nations. These are particularly complex issues and the forces of opposition will be fierce. But the point is that any post-growth transition is going to require deep changes to the most fundamental banking, monetary, and financial institutions of capitalism.
- *Population Policies*: This is always controversial territory, especially in an age of rising social polarisation, but the environmental logic is compel-

ling. As a population grows, more resources are required to provide for the material conditions of human wellbeing. As Paul Ehrlich once said: 'Whatever problem you're interested in, you're not going to solve it unless you also solve the population problem.' We won't pose specific policies. The point is that this topic needs to be discussed openly and with wisdom and compassion. Equitable population policies must be part of any coherent politics of sustainability in recognition that we live on a 'full Earth'. Nevertheless, population must not be used as a scapegoat to deflect attention away from the more fundamental problem of unsustainable affluence and the political economies of growth that both drive and require unsustainable consumption (see Harvey 1974).

- *Distributive Justice*: As noted earlier, environmental concerns cannot be isolated from social justice concerns, both nationally and globally. Prominent policies in this space include the notion of a Universal Basic Income, while others argue for a job guarantee or Universal Basic Services. These types of policies would go a long way to directly eliminating poverty, with funding supported by a maximum wage, wealth taxes, and land taxes that sought to reduce inequality. Again, ecosocialists would argue that a just distribution of wealth and power would have to involve significant socialisation of property and curtailment of 'the market'. How far socialisation would need to go, and the nature of such a transformation, is obviously open to debate.

These policy platforms—all in need of elaboration and discussion—are sound guiding goals if a transition to degrowth society were recognised as necessary. Each of these policies could take various forms, and there is, and should be, debate within the degrowth movement and beyond about various ways to structure a post-capitalist society. But our present point is simply that a coherent alternative politico-economic project is emerging to replace the capitalist paradigm. So, the second prerequisite for a paradigm shift is also arguably present, which is to say: viable and desirable alternative structures exist. Capitalist realism—the belief that there is no alternative to the existing political economy—is a dangerous illusion.

Nevertheless, as implied above, we are the first to admit that this policy platform, coherent though it may be, is so unpalatable to the dominant cultural consciousness that it would essentially be political suicide for any political party to try to implement it at present. In other words, what is arguably politically necessary is both socially and politically unthinkable, which is one reason, no doubt, for the current state of despairing political paralysis.

Because of this situation, whereby the politically necessary is almost unthinkable, we would argue that the policy platform outlined is unlikely to *initiate* a degrowth transition but will only ever be the *outcome* of social movements: the product, that is, of social forces that emerge out of crisis or a series of crises and which actively create the cultural consciousness that see policies for degrowth as both necessary and desirable (Alexander and Gleeson 2019). It is through crisis that we see the citizenries in affluent societies being awakened from the depoliticising effects of affluence. Encountering crises can play, and might have to play, an essential consciousness-raising role, if it triggers a desire to learn about the structural underpinnings of the crisis situation itself.

While we do not deny the need for, and desirability of, deep structural changes in the nature of our economic and political systems, what we are proposing is that a post-capitalist government may only be the outcome, not the driving force, of a transition to a just and sustainable society. In other words, our best hope for inducing a degrowth transition by design is to build a post-capitalist economics 'from below', within the shell of the current system that is currently in the process of deteriorating. Waiting for governments would be like waiting for Godot—a tragicomedy in two acts, in which nothing happens, twice.

Support from a Comprehensive Coalition of Social Forces

This leads to the third prerequisite for a degrowth transition: that it must have support from a comprehensive coalition of social forces. Again, space does not permit an in-depth review of these issues. Instead, a few comments will be made on examples of post-capitalist grassroots activities that are exploring modes of economy that are transcending the profit-motive for the common good, or simply building new forms of informal or household economies 'beyond the market'. These can easily be seen to be prefiguring aspects of a degrowth economy, even if this terminology is not always used. Below we state four key features of post-capitalism that we see emerging from the grassroots up, features which we feel must scale up for a degrowth economy to emerge:

- First, non-monetary forms of the sharing economy, whereby communities self-organise to share resources in order to save money, partially 'escape the market', and avoid significant amounts of production. Indeed, this is a key feature of why a degrowth economy could still thrive even when contracting: produce much less but share much more. This is part of what efficiency means in a degrowth economy. Societies can create common wealth through sharing.
- Second, a degrowth economy is likely to require a transformation of the household economy, away from merely being a place of consumption and into a place of production and self-provision. On this topic there is no better place to look than the work of permaculturist David Holmgren (2018), whose vision and insights here are indispensable. There are two main reasons why a resurgence of household economies is central to a degrowth paradigm shift (Alexander and Gleeson 2019). First, by producing more within the household, less time is needed to work in the formal economy, leaving more time outside the market for social activism and community engagement. This strategy is about escaping capitalism in order to erode it, thereby building the new economy within the shell of the old. Secondly, if financial crises deepen in coming years, the household economy may be an essential means of meeting basic needs, so the task is to prepare now for what may well prove to be harder economic times ahead.
- A third key feature of a degrowth economy involves significant localisation of the economy, moving toward a 'bioregional' economy where local needs are predominantly met with local resources, shortening the chain between production and consumption (Trainer 2010; Norberg-Hodge 2019).
- Finally, we'll note that any post-capitalist economy is going to require new modes of production, moving away from profit-maximising corporations which are often owned by absentee shareholders, towards an

economy where worker cooperatives, community enterprises, and not-for-profit models are the dominant forms of economic organisation, paying people living wages but reinvesting surpluses back into the community (Gibson-Graham et al. 2013). Again, there are various ways to imagine such alternative economic arrangements. Experimentation will be required as societies pursue the goal of creating economic and social systems in which more wealth and power are held in common, rather than concentrating it in private hands.

It seems to us that these alternative modes of economy, and many more besides, are bubbling everywhere under the surface, which is a hopeful sign. But one must also admit that often these transgressive experiments remain small and marginalised by the dominant modes of economy. So, in terms of the third prerequisite for a post-capitalist transition, we might have to conclude that the social forces are mobilising but have not yet been able to scale up to positively disrupt, or even significantly threaten, the dominant paradigm.

Cultural Consent: The Sufficiency Imperative

The final prerequisite for a post-capitalist degrowth transition is broad-based cultural consent. Passive consent may suffice here, without the majority of people actively seeking degrowth. This really is a critical element in any planned transition in political economy and one that currently does not exist in terms of degrowth. It seems that the majority of people either do not think degrowth (or what it represents) is necessary or, if they do, they do not like what it means in terms of reduced and transformed consumption and production practices.

We think there are two main reasons why culture is not ready to embrace degrowth. The first reason is a deep-seated techno-optimism that shapes cultural thinking about environmental problems. This view assumes that technology and market mechanisms will be able to resolve the crises of capitalism without system change and without even much in terms of lifestyle change. In other words, the zeitgeist of our times seems to be that consumer affluence is consistent with justice and sustainability, because it is assumed that efficiency improvements in modes of production will be able to produce 'green growth' without having to rethink consumption practices (Hickel and Kallis 2019).

Although this techno-optimistic blind spot is a major obstacle to degrowth, we hold some uneasy confidence that as capitalism continues to collide with ecological limits in coming years and decades, the case for degrowth will only become clearer to more and more people, which could act as a mobilising force.

However, even if the crises of capitalism deepen and the majority of people come to desire a post-capitalist political economy, it does not follow that a degrowth economy is what they would demand (Buch-Hansen 2018). This points to a serious cultural obstacle to a degrowth transition. It seems to us that there will never be a post-capitalist politics until there is a post-consumerist culture that is prepared to embrace material sufficiency as a desirable way of life. Herein lies the instructive importance of the voluntary simplicity, simple living, and downshifting movements, and their pre-existing manifestations in traditional and Indigenous ways of living. Although many of these contemporary social movements are in need of radicalisation and organisation for collective action, these counter currents are beginning to create the cultural conditions needed for a politics and economics beyond capitalism to emerge. The great dissolution of capitalism is underway. It is already time for new imaginaries to begin the work of reconstruction.

References

Alexander, Samuel, and Josh Floyd. 2018. *Carbon Civilisation and the Energy Descent Future: Life Beyond this Brief Anomaly.* Melbourne: Simplicity Institute.

Alexander, Samuel, and Brendan Gleeson. 2019. *Degrowth in the Suburbs: A Radical Urban Imaginary.* Singapore: Palgrave Macmillan.

Buch-Hansen, Hubert. 2018. The Prerequisites for a Degrowth Paradigm Shift: Insights from Critical Political Economy. *Ecological Economics* 146: 157–163.

Gibson-Graham, J.K., Jenny Cameron, and Stephen Healy. 2013. *Take Back the Economy: An Ethical Guide for Transforming Our Communities.* Minneapolis: University of Minnesota Press.

Hamblin, James. 2016. How Cubans Live as Long as Americans at a Tenth of the Cost. *The Atlantic*, November 30.

Harvey, David. 1974. Population, Resources, and the Ideology of Science. *Economic Geography* 50 (3): 256–277.

Hickel, Jason, and Giorgos Kallis. 2019. Is Green Growth Possible? *New Political Economy* (in press). Published online 17 April 2019.

Holmgren, David. 2018. *RetroSuburbia: The Downshifter's Guide to a Resilient Future*. Hepburn Springs: Melliodora Publishing.

Norberg-Hodge, Helena. 2019. *Local is Our Future: Steps to an Economics of Happiness*. Byron Bay: Local Futures.

Smith, Richard. 2016. *Green Capitalism: The God that Failed*. London: College Publications.

Trainer, Ted. 2010. *Transition to a Sustainable and Just World*. Sydney: Envirobook.

6

China: Capitalism and Change?

Michael Webber

The geographic centre of the global economy has shifted dramatically since 1950. Led first by Japan, Korea, and Taiwan, the People's Republic of China is now the centre of this transformation: according to the World Bank, its share of global production has risen from less than 2 per cent in 1980 to about 15 per cent now (in USD; the shift is even greater if measured in purchasing power). Producers in China have become the most important cogs in the wheels of the global capitalist economy—and they are poised to become even more important, shaping not only the volume of global production but also the forms that it takes. Likewise, the Chinese government has become one of the most important players in forming the institutions and infrastructures of global capitalism, and thus in framing the livelihood prospects of people all over the world.

People, institutions, and governments outside China have devoted vast amounts of time and enormous numbers of pages of books, journals, and newspapers commenting on how the rise of China poses a threat to global

M. Webber (✉)
School of Geography, Earth and Atmospheric Sciences, University of Melbourne, Parkville, VIC, Australia

capitalism, offers opportunities for further capitalist growth, or promises to change some of the rules that underpin the global capitalist enterprise. There are remarkably few published imaginations of the future in Chinese. Hong Kong popular culture is obsessed with the struggles for cultural autonomy between local, Chinese, and global sources of power; it includes both utopian and dystopian visions (Wu, H. 2020b). On the mainland, mainstream political debates have shifted from a legitimacy-criticising imaginary that is grounded within the party-state's 'reform framework' towards a discourse of competition between civilisations that is increasingly nationalist, racialized, and illiberal (Wu, A.X. 2020a; Zhang 2020). Unease at the human and environmental burdens imposed on rural people by the urban, capitalist economy spurred New Rural Reconstruction (NRR) movements, but these are now largely subsumed within the government's rhetoric of a New Socialist Countryside. Either authoritarian government has efficiently erased almost all public statements of enthusiasm for an alternative future or else current systems remain popular.

The governors of China hold ambivalent views about capitalism and its existence in their country: capitalism is 'do, but don't say'; 'signal left, turn right'; 'ever present, but unsaid'; even officially denied. While inclined to accept that China is (to some extent) capitalist, political economists are ambivalent about the extent of capitalist social relations in China, about the markers of Chinese particularity, and about the sources of its capitalist dynamics (Arrighi 2009; Harvey 2005; Peck and Zhang 2013). What then is the nature of this thing that portends such changes to global capitalism?

Capitalist production in China is the same as capitalist production everywhere else. It's a form of production in which money is advanced to purchase raw materials, plant and equipment, and labour power with the intention of selling a product that earns more money than was initially advanced. It entails certain preconditions: there exists money, there exist markets at least for the necessary raw materials, plant and equipment, and for the final product, and there are markets in which labourers offer for sale their capacity to work (their labour power). The final product might be a car, an advertisement, or even advice. Such a form of production is widespread in China—in private corporations, in many state-owned enterprises (SOEs), and in foreign-invested enterprises. The status of SOEs is complex and debated. The government through the State-owned Assets Supervision and Administration Commission of the State Council (SASAC) owns the large central government SOEs, and similar bodies own SOEs at provincial and lower levels of government; senior executives are hired and fired by the SASAC. The government expects them to make profits; indeed, China's National Bureau of Statistics estimates that in 2018 the profits of SOEs were equivalent to about 6 per cent of total industrial value added. Gong (2018) illustrates how such corporations navigate between the demands of profitability and government policy.

What is distinctive about capitalism in any society is the way in which capitalist production interacts with other forms of production and with other social institutions. By far, the largest and most important system of production is the Earth: it supplies the trees, rivers, minerals, animals, and air on which we all survive. The different human ways of organising production in China include several hundred million petty commodity producers (peasant farmers and small shopkeepers) who principally rely on themselves and their household members to produce goods for sale in a market, and a large sector of not-for-profit government and quasi-government agencies (such as charities, public hospitals, schools, universities, and utilities). The largest non-capitalist sector in China, as elsewhere, is the household sector—the activities inside a dwelling through which food is prepared, clothing is kept clean, children are raised. These are the most prevalent methods of production in China, and capitalists exploit all of them to provide an expanding supply of appropriately skilled and healthy workers, to supply raw materials, and to act as a market for the commodities that they produce. Wherever we live, most of us are familiar with these kinds of interaction between capitalist and other forms of production and with the thought processes that imagine 'production' as only capitalist production.

More distinctive in China is the manner in which capitalists interact with other social institutions, including government bureaucracies and political institutions. In North America, Western Europe, Japan, South Korea, and Australia/New Zealand (which for brevity I'll call 'the West'), we're used to the fact that capitalist interests have a powerful place at the political table, leading to a generalised, if not universal, acceptance of capitalist ways of organising, especially among the political elite. These places are not identical: France and West Germany have more powerful unions and government actors than the USA or UK, for example. In Japan and South Korea, during their periods of rapid industrialisation and capital formation, politicians and bureaucracies created specific and productive relationships with newly emerging capitalist corporations. Since the 1990s, in both countries, corporate-political-bureaucratic relationships have become more like those in Western Europe. But the political party and government bureaucracies in China have quite different interactions with capitalists than do political parties or bureaucracies in the West. In other words, specificity comes from the different ways in which capitalist production interacts (is articulated) with other ways of organising society.

Opinions differ about what these specificities might be. For some, China is distinguished by what Habermas (1987) called the life-world: the shared common understandings and values of Chinese people. Chinese writers identify pursuit of material self-interest; social relations that are ordered by personal ties of family, locality, education, and the like; formal obedience to secular authority and status; and pragmatic strategies of concrete action. However, these characteristics are not important constraints on the behaviour of capitalists, features that might undo capitalism in China, nor do they pose significant threats to global capitalism. For others, hukou and the absence of privately owned land, remnants of the era of Mao, differentiate China from the West. (Hukou is a system of citizenship-by-birthplace that restricts the life chances of people born in rural areas and small cities.) These 'non-capitalist' remnants are gradually disappearing; notably, though land is not privately owned, use rights in land can now be privately owned and traded. Hukou and the state ownership of land are significant for individuals, but not for the system of capitalist production.

Two other attributes seem more important—authoritarianism and the role of the Chinese Communist Party (CCP) and governments in economic life. Over issues of perceived national security, such as independence movements in Xinjiang and Tibet/Xizang, pro-democracy movements in Hong Kong, or movements that claim authority separate from the CCP (such as Falun Gong or the Dalai Lama), the central government is able to exert direct, coercive power. There have been periods of widespread dissent since the revolution of 1949, including the Beijing Spring of 1978 and the Tiananmen Square protests of 1989, there are widespread single-issue demonstrations, and there exist well-known (in the West at least) pro-democracy activists. However, the tools of repression coupled with an ideological claim about the 'need for stability' seem for now able to contain such threats to authoritarian rule. Outside direct threats to security, commentators agree that Chinese authoritarianism is fragmented, subject to discontinuities in the chains of command from the central government to local governments and to poor coordination between the governments of differing jurisdictions and between departments within the same jurisdiction (Lieberthal and Oksenberg 1988). In some respects, decentralisation and fragmentation encourage innovations in policy, as successful social experiments in one locality are copied and generalised by the central government: the dissolution of communal farming, the system of responsibility for river health, and the system of local 'Silicon Valleys' all originated in local experiments. In other respects, fragmentation has bedevilled the central government's attempts to assert its authority in order to control pollution and to limit urban encroachment on agricultural land.

Capitalist production inside China occurs within private enterprises, international corporations, and SOEs. There are also joint ventures between international and Chinese private enterprises or SOEs. Private and international corporations are only allowed to operate within a restricted range of industries. Increasingly in private enterprises like Huawei, Xiaomi, DJI, Alibaba, Tencent, and Baidu, the CCP has committees at levels from the shop floor up to senior executives with the right to participate in decision making, and there are moves to expand the CCP's influence within international companies. The role of the government and Party within SOEs is more overt: the government through the SASAC owns the large central government SOEs, and similar bodies own SOEs at provincial and lower levels of government; senior executives are hired and fired by the SASAC, and the CCP committees within the corporations have long-established roles. Since Xi Jinping came to power in 2012, the CCP's influence over all these corporations has increased.

But this relationship is not simply one way. All these corporations—private, international, and state-owned—depend on profits to fuel capital accumulation. Concerns in the West about authoritarianism and the CCP's influence over corporations have harmed some of them, as the disputes over Huawei's participation in the construction of 5G networks illustrates. Equally, the 'China Goes Out' policy reflects both a political need to expand China's influence and an economic need to find larger markets and wider sources of supply to feed accumulation. Furthermore, while some CCP or government officials assume high office in SOEs, the reverse is also true—enterprise managers move into CCP or government positions. The structural imperative, to sustain rates of accumulation through profits, provides a power through which corporations can resist CCP or government interference: capitalist corporations are an actual alternative source of power in China.

So far, these two sources of power—the CCP and capitalists—have co-existed in an environment of rapid growth, fuelled by the continuing migration of low-paid workers from the countryside and a form of inter-regional competition that has unleashed world-leading rates of technical innovation. The government controls trade unions and suppresses independent forms of worker dissent. It offers diplomatic support to corporations that are in trouble overseas. And it is using huge projects, such as the Belt and Road Initiative, alongside new international development funds, to support Chinese firms as they seek markets for construction projects outside China (Han and Webber 2020).

However, these golden-age conditions are changing. Internally, the rate of capital accumulation depends on the rate of growth of capitalist GDP and the share of that accruing as profits. The profit share depends on wages (i.e., on the suppression of worker's demands by authority or by competition from underemployed migrant workers) and the share of non-wage corporate income that is extracted as rent, taxes, and the like (i.e., principally, on state extraction). Equally, the rate of growth of capitalist GDP depends on the growth of the labour force working for capitalist firms, the rate of productivity change, the rate of growth of net exports, and the rate of growth of government spending on items that are fulfilled by capitalist production (such as infrastructure construction). Rates of growth of export markets and the labour force are both decelerating; and the government cannot continuously increase the rate of growth of infrastructure spending. Under such conditions, high rates of accumulation depend on slow growth in wages, lowered state extractions from profits, and high rates of productivity change—that is on expanding state support for capitalist forms of production. Here lie the seeds of a more strained relationship between the CCP and capitalist producers.

Provided that the nationalist ambitions of the CCP and many Chinese people to export China's model of development, to grow export markets, and to assert a greater political role in running the world economy do not lead to destructive conflict with other countries, either the CCP will have to cede authority to the class of capitalist producers (i.e., adopt policies to maximise the rate of economic growth) or else capitalists will have to submit to continuing and expanded control by the CCP. The former looks like authoritarian capitalism, perhaps focused on extending the rules of a market economy and even merging onto a path like that of Japan or South Korea after World War II. The Hu Jintao/Wen Jiabao regime appeared to be veering towards this authoritarian capitalist path, but Xi Jinping has reclaimed more authority for the CCP (and himself). The path of expanded CCP control resembles a state-dominated organisation of large-scale production surrounded by Earth processes, petty commodity producers, a large sector of not-for-profit government and quasi-government agencies, and capitalist producers. This is one post-capitalist future for China.

The Earth is another source of power that is outside political and economic control, a power that arises from its contribution to production and wellbeing. In China, this power is manifest as environmental deterioration. Air, soil, and water pollution in China are generally sufficiently high to pose dangers to health; efforts to prevent further deterioration are likely to raise costs of production. Floods and droughts have for centuries posed threats to people's lives and wellbeing and continue to do so. And above all of these is, of course, climate change, which threatens as-yet-unforeseen changes to the conditions of life and production. The government's methods of remedying pollution, reducing the risks posed by floods and drought, and ameliorating the rate of climate change commonly involve large amounts of concrete and machinery, serving only to grow the markets of capitalist producers. A major incident, such as a flood along the Yellow River or a dam failing, *would* pose a severe threat to the authority of the CCP; barring such events, environmental remediation is for now an opportunity for capitalist producers.

The exercise of authority by the Earth, despite China's particular issues of environmental management, principally revolves around climate change. Imaginaries of future paths in the face of climatic change include continued reliance on fossil fuels, apocalypse, a techno-market form of ecological modernisation, and sustainable lifestyles of various forms (Levy and Spicer 2013). A fossil-fuelled future supposes that the climate system is less fragile than climate scientists now believe: it presages a future that merges into apocalypse. The government is promising and actively planning to wean China off its reliance on fossil fuels. The imaginary of sustainable lifestyles assumes that the climate system is fragile and that radical changes need to be made to capitalist production to achieve sustainability. Despite plans for eco-cities and experiments in more sustainable forms of rural livelihood (promulgated by the NRR movement), there is little to indicate that localised, non-capitalist, sustainable lifestyles can wriggle free of the CCP's dominance. A techno-market solution foresees merely more climate-friendly forms of production that are entirely compatible with current systems of production, including capitalism. Within China, the techno-market solution of ecological modernisation is the official stance of the government, supported by increasing government-led investment, and rather grandly called 'ecological civilisation'; provided that apocalypse does not happen and that the government continues to support large-scale environmental remediation, this path only portends a state-led, more environmentally friendly form of capitalist production.

The third seed of social change within China is armed or cyber conflict with other countries. China's expanding geopolitical and military power is increasingly in conflict with US assumptions of global hegemony. In spite of the rhetoric of 'China's peaceful rise', the relations between China and some of its neighbours are poor: there are (sometimes armed) conflicts with India over their border; the status of Taiwan and China's territorial claims over the South China Sea are provoking disputes with Vietnam, the Philippines, as well as the US and its allies. Conflicts with other countries lead to futures that are entirely unpredictable: warlordism, civil war, a crime wave, proliferation of nuclear weapons have all been mentioned (Xia, n.d.).

This analysis suggests that there are several possible paths for China: a kind of soft authoritarian capitalism, perhaps with market-led pro-environment policies; state-dominated organisation of large-scale production, perhaps with state-led ecological modernisation; and a dystopian future that involves more serious calamities than the mere future of capitalism. Whatever the precise future, households, petty commodity producers, not-for-profits, and the Earth will continue to make the largest contributions to output; capitalist production, even if not dominant, will also continue in some form. Despite the logic of this analysis, it is likely that any substantial deviation from capitalist production in China will arise from some event or series of events that are not for now seen as significant.

References

Arrighi, Giovanni. 2009. *Adam Smith in Beijing*. London: Verso.
Gong, Xue. 2018. The Role of Chinese Corporate Players in China's South China Sea policy. *Contemporary Southeast Asia: A Journal of International and Strategic Affairs* 40: 301–326.
Habermas, Jurgen. 1987. *The Theory of Communicative Action, Vol 2: Life-World and System*. Boston: Beacon Press.
Han, Xiao, and Michael Webber. 2020. From Chinese Dam Building in Africa to the Belt and Road Initiative: Assembling Infrastructure Projects and Their Linkages. *Political Geography* 77. https://doi.org/10.1016/j.polgeo.2019.102102.
Harvey, David. 2005. *A Brief History of Neoliberalism*. New York: Oxford University Press.
Levy, David L., and Andre Spicer. 2013. Contested Imaginaries and the Cultural Political Economy of Climate Change. *Organization* 20 (5): 659–678.
Lieberthal, Kenneth, and Michel Oksenberg. 1988. *Policy Making in China: Leaders, Structures, and Processes*. Princeton, NJ: Princeton University Press.
Peck, Jamie, and Jun Zhang. 2013. A Variety of Capitalism … with Chinese Characteristics? *Journal of Economic Geography* 13 (3): 357–396.

Wu, Angela Xiao. 2020a. The Evolution of Regime Imaginaries on the Chinese Internet. *Journal of Political Ideologies* 25 (2): 139–161.

Wu, Helena. 2020b. Imagining the Future in Post-millennial Hong Kong Cinema: Visualizing the Local, the National and the Global in Cultural Imaginaries. *Journal of Chinese Cinemas* 14 (1): 32–49.

Xia, Ming. n.d. "China threat" or "peaceful rise of China"? *New York Times, College*. Accessed October 05, 2020. https://archive.nytimes.com/www.nytimes.com/ref/college/coll-china-politics-007.html.

Zhang, Chenchen. 2020. Right-wing Populism with Chinese Characteristics? Identity, Otherness and Global Imaginaries in Debating World Politics Online. *European Journal of International Relations* 26 (1): 88–115.

Part II

Governing for Post-Capitalist Futures

7

From Technological Utopianism to Universal Basic Services

Boris Frankel

Across the political spectrum, policy analysts, radicals, businesses, and governments have been seduced by the belief that new technologies will solve the environmental unsustainability of incessant capitalist growth or enable post-capitalist societies to provide 'fully automated luxury communism' for all (Aaron Bastani 2019). Pro-capitalist policy makers are hoping that technological innovation will help fend off calls for substantial reforms and thwart any possibility for a radical post-capitalist future to emerge. The aim is to ensure endless growth in capitalist production and consumption by absolutely decoupling economic growth from the ecological constraints of finite natural resources. To date, no country has managed to decouple economic growth from environmental impacts. The latest analyses of whether decoupling exists (Parrique et al. 2019), including 179 reports that claimed decoupling (Vadén et al. 2020), found

B. Frankel (✉)
Melbourne Institute of Sustainable Society, University of Melbourne, Parkville, VIC, Australia
e-mail: boris.frankel@unimelb.edu.au

that even 'relative decoupling' in select industries has been extremely difficult to achieve and is non-existent across entire capitalist economies.

Whether imaginative solutions are proposed by defenders or opponents of capitalist market societies, the test of any proposal is not its theoretical allure but rather its political, economic, social, and environmental feasibility. Even having political power has proved insufficient, as it is the height of human arrogance to think that we can control nature permanently to serve our needs. Undeterred, utopian schemes keep appearing. Jeremy Rifkin is one such prominent optimist. Consultant to governments, businesses, and trade unions, Rifkin straddles both Right and centre-Left with his notion of the 'zero marginal cost' economy (2014). This new system will consist of three operating engines: first, a communication network based on the 'internet of things'; second, a sustainable energy system driven by renewables; and third, a new mobility and logistics system based on driverless vehicles circulating goods made by 3D printers. By 2030, Rifkin envisages hundreds of millions of buildings producing their own decentralised energy from renewable solar and wind sources. Instead of a top-down, centralised economic system, there will be 100 trillion sensors in the world facilitating the three operating engines that connect the entire human race. People will thus by-pass corporations and governments and engage directly with one another as a 'collaborative commons'.

Unfortunately, Rifkin lacks a politics with which to explain how his imaginary world can be realised. Zero marginal cost production rests on the myth of 'free' and assumes that the cost of producing the original product is zero or near zero, and that all subsequent copies can be produced without cost by digital and other three-dimensional additive manufacturing. This scenario completely ignores the 'hardware' of information technology which is produced by low-paid workers in developing countries and also ignores the mountain of e-waste that is very difficult to recycle or safely dispose. Although zero marginal cost production has partially happened in publishing, music, and information, Rifkin claims that it can be extended to all goods via the 'internet of things'. Somehow, steel furnaces, heavy engineering for infrastructure, millions of houses, and billions of electric self-driving cars by 2050 can all be miraculously made by 3D printers that do not deplete natural resources or use fossil fuel-based polymers. Like many utopian market entrepreneurs, Rifkin's world is unconstrained by scarcity or the need for products to either make profits or create the revenue required to maintain vital services in a post-capitalist world. There is little recognition of the limits and inadequacies of technology in female-dominated care services such as nursing, child rearing, and aged care. All will be free and automated, yet somehow, millions of new jobs will be created. It is an utterly inconsistent and fiscally, environmentally, and politically unsustainable vision.

Socialist radicals to the left of Rifkin are also seduced by the promise of new technology. While the radical Left is extremely weak in developed capitalist countries, utopian thinking flourishes to fill the gap created by the absence of strong mass movements. Paradoxically, the fewer possibilities of radical change, the more elaborate and excessive the utopian visions become. A false optimism is created as radical Accelerationists in the UK and Left Promethean writers in the US attack many environmentalists for supposedly offering nothing but 'eco-austerity' (Frase et al. 2017). Instead, they promote hyper-technological solutions including nuclear power, dangerous geo-engineering, discredited carbon capture, and the old Promethean goal of controlling nature. Take away private ownership of wealth and power and there is little difference between the faith these radicals have in techno-fixes and similar corporate capitalist technological panaceas.

Journalist Paul Mason (2015) has done much to popularise the notion of 'post-capitalism'. He also subscribes to the 'zero marginal cost society'. There is a chasm between his penetrating critique of capitalism and the flimsy character of his post-capitalist proposals. Nearly all his post-capitalist examples come from digital media and simply fail to translate adequately when applied to key areas of mining, manufacturing, and food production. Mason uncritically accepts the ecological modernisation ideology of 'green growth'. Given that half of the world's population is *not* online, especially the global poor, Mason's post-capitalist alternative to neoliberalism lacks a plausible political economy of transition. To hundreds of millions of people who do not even have electricity or running water, the 'zero marginal cost society' remains in the realm of fantasy.

Media blogger Aaron Bastani (2019) goes one step further than Mason by proclaiming 'fully automated luxury communism' (FALC). He synthesises the ideas of the Left Prometheans, Accelerationists such as Nick Srnicek and Alex Williams (2016), who demand full automation combined with a universal basic income (UBI), and other radical currents. Bastani sees new technologies liberating us from work and creating a world of abundance, luxury, and happiness. His book is like a 'boys own manual', featuring everything from the colonisation of planets to the creation of a post-work society. Although invoking environmental issues, the notion that everyone can live a life of material abundance enjoyed by billionaires is deeply delusional and regressive, especially in a time when production and consumption have already damaged many ecosystems. I agree with Bastani that reducing the working week and the radical redistribution of resources are vital. Yet, tellingly, Bastani's vision of utopian abundance shows little awareness that technology cannot magically overcome environmental constraints. However, Bastani is cautious when it comes to popular but problematic solutions such as UBI and instead supports the need for universal basic services (UBS).

A growing number of neo-Keynesian analysts such as the Social Prosperity Network (2017) and Anna Coote et al. (2019) put forward a social-democratic UBS. Instead of conventional incremental welfare state changes, I believe a UBS offers the best viable alternative political strategy for any radical transition to post-capitalist societies (Frankel 2018, 2020). Given mass unemployment, deep social inequality, and major environmental and economic crises, a broad UBS strategy is an answer to both existing failed or inadequate capitalist welfare regimes and environmentally unsustainable capitalist growth. Combatting unemployment with conventional private employment that fuels consumer booms is ecologically unsustainable. By contrast, a UBS will assist in the necessary reduction and/or redistribution of material resources. It will do this by shifting the present emphasis on mainly money wages to a higher percentage of reward in the form of comprehensive social wages, such as healthcare, housing, public transport, and a range of social needs. Currently, in OECD countries with more developed welfare provisions such as France or Norway, approximately 20 per cent to 30 per cent of household income comes from state-provided benefits. Lifting this to at least 50 per cent of household income over a transitional period would fundamentally alter the balance between market commodified wage labour and decommodified non-market social services. Also, most of these social wage services would not have the same level of material, carbon, and water footprints as major industries such as the massive automobile sector.

The old dilemma of how to fund degrowth and social welfare systems that depend on the revenue derived from the growth of unsustainable commodity production is partially solved by developing a UBS. Although UBS schemes would not initially become independent of capitalist production, the growth of employment in the 'social' green sectors and the 'care economy' would simultaneously generate taxation from employees and help change patterns of consumption and over-reliance on private service providers. Currently, the proportion of household consumption of durable goods (like cars or whitegoods) in relation to non-durable goods (food, fuel, and clothing) and services (private services such as telecommunications, health, insurance, personal care, tourism) has changed in developed countries over the past fifty years. More services and fewer durable goods are consumed annually. A UBS could push this historical trend in the direction of more publicly provided decommodified services, less imported goods, and other measures to help make individual per capita and national material, carbon, water, and other resources more ecologically sustainable.

Universal basic services require interventionist states with enhanced capacities to help plan, co-ordinate, fund, and implement many facets of a UBS strategy. I am not referring to existing centralised and monolithic state apparatuses. Instead, there are many ideas about how to introduce new conceptions of the relationship between UBS and what other theorists call the 'foundational economy'. This group of theorists (Bentham et al. 2013) in Manchester, Barcelona, London, and other cities start with the following premises: firstly, central governments should not abdicate responsibility and leave cities and regions suffering from decades of under-development to deal with inequality and lack of resources. However, given most central national governments' lack the imagination and knowledge to deal with local and regional problems, it is necessary to reinvent, empower, and develop the micro-level capacities of local and regional governments who are most familiar with their own needs in regard to employment, services, industries, and ecology. Secondly, instead of beginning with abstract concepts of 'the market' or an 'undifferentiated capitalism', it is crucial to recognise that the basic materials of everyday life 'are exceptionally diverse in their production cycles, their economic geographies, the complexity of their inputs, their spatial relations and reliance on land...' (Hall and Schafran 2017: 8)

Thirdly, rather than focus on the tradeable and competitive parts of the production system, as if they were the 'whole economy', the 'foundational economy approach' divides each local, regional, and national economy into zones. The tradeable and competitive market businesses are only one zone. The other zones consist of the family or household core zone, the essential services zone in health, education, transport, housing, energy, and so forth, and the occasional zone of activities such as holidays and haircuts. While all of the Foundational Economy group are not geared to radical post-capitalist change, they do overlap with advocates of UBS in emphasising the need to develop essential services and especially those zones of regional and local economies that shift the social and economic activity away from commercial tradeable commodities to decommodified services, employment, and infrastructure. This would help reduce poverty and inequality, especially gender inequality and lack of support for women as the main care providers, in ways compatible with environmental sustainability.

Importantly, in every country, UBS proposals are immediately aimed at those most in need. In contrast to universal income schemes that indiscriminately provide all individuals with the same income regardless of personal wealth and income, a UBS would initially prioritise lifting the quality of life for the bottom 30 per cent to 50 per cent of low- and middle-income people in OECD countries and 60 per cent to 75 per cent of people in low- and middle-income countries. Far too many people suffer needlessly, die prematurely, or are incapacitated due to lack of physical, dental, and mental health care. Homelessness and sub-standard accommodation are widespread. Essential utilities such as electricity, running water, sewerage, or safe urban living conditions free of violence, toxic pollution, and industrial noise should be provided to all people as well as minimal levels of greenery and recreational spaces. Contemporary education, employment, and social interaction require access to telecommunication facilities and a good public transport system. While all people would be eligible for services, preference would first be given to those who could not afford privately run services and have no access to essential public services because none exist, are in short supply, or are grossly underfunded and understaffed.

Compared to the prohibitively expensive cost of an austere UBI, the provision of a range of essential services would be relatively cheap and much more effective. For example, instead of spending US$3 trillion per annum on a sub-poverty level UBI of US$10,000 per year in the US, the equivalent amount or even $2 trillion per year on basic services would lead to dramatic improvements in the quality-of-care services, housing, and healthcare over a short period. Twenty to 30 trillion dollars of additional expenditure over a decade would deliver a vastly improved social state for tens of millions of low- and middle-income Americans. Similar levels of expenditure as a proportion of GDP in dozens of countries would also dramatically improve the quality of life for more than five billion people living without adequate basic services.

Importantly, UBI schemes provide no assurance that individuals will stop living highly individualistic lives. By contrast, UBS programs are more likely to promote social co-operation and solidarity because the improvement and creation of essential services simultaneously provides jobs in many care sectors while raising the quality of life for the recipients and undercutting the market provision of these services that currently millions of people cannot afford. Conversely, UBI schemes will not improve essential services. Instead, due to the high cost of income schemes, the establishment of good, universally accessible public health and social care systems in the many countries that currently lack these services would be undermined. Should expensive but austere sub-poverty level UBI schemes be adopted, post-capitalism will remain just as distant, and millions would still not be able to afford healthcare and other basic services. While a UBS will not be cheap, it will not create major political divisions amongst workers. Unlike the divisiveness of a UBI, UBS will benefit many workers directly and indirectly. An improved social wage would also facilitate political coalitions between the recipients of essential services and those who pay the taxes for these services because many will simultaneously be taxpayers and beneficiaries of an improved social wage.

COVID-19 has shown that despite crucial government income supplements for workers in lockdown at home, basic income has not prevented an increase in domestic violence and abuse, mental illness, and racism. The lesson here is that a UBI would do very little to change either dominant masculinist values or prevent the reproduction of existing socio-cultural disadvantages. Income-only alternatives such as UBI schemes would still leave people without desperately needed community infrastructure such as childcare, housing, public transport, healthcare, and other vital support services. By contrast, comprehensive UBS provisions would help counter the isolation and burden of carers otherwise left to cope alone at home with only a sub-poverty-level UBI. The illusion that such minimal UBI payments would reduce gender inequality without an extensive support network of basic services is one held mainly by those in the affluent middle-class who live comfortable lives and do not know what it is like to survive on inadequate or no welfare services.

The UBS has many strengths but it would have much greater impact if it were linked to a job guarantee program, with governments offering decent wages to all who voluntarily desired to work. Radically, it would eliminate unemployment and under-employment. In contrast to those advocates who propose paying minimum wage rates to workers on job guarantee, I believe that all prospective workers should be given the choice of either full-time or part-time work with prevailing minimum wage rates being only the floor-level rates. Instead, during the transition to post-capitalism, 'job guarantee' workers should be paid similar rates to others with skills or professional qualifications. A UBS scheme would complement a full employment society by reducing the length of the paid working week, shifting the home-work balance in a meaningful way by simultaneously supplementing low money wages and over-worked people with more free time and a vastly improved range of *social wage* services. However, if privatised or outsourced to private contractors, full employment would not necessarily decommodify social relations. Hence, the higher percentage of the work-age population employed in public job guarantee programs, the higher the level of decommodification of market-determined wage relations. If 10 per cent to 25 per cent of a country's workforce were initially freed from competitive labour market conditions, this could give workers employed in private sector businesses greater political bargaining strength. Stagnant wages and deteriorating work conditions over the past thirty years have been made possible in many countries by high unemployment and under-employment levels. Eliminating unemployment, under-employment, and precarity through a job guarantee would thus restore the capacity of workers to face employers on a more equal footing. Newly employed 'job guarantee' workers will simultaneously help deliver and also benefit from the expanded UBS programmes at national, regional, and local levels. They will, very importantly, help cover part of the cost of a job guarantee and UBS by earning wages and paying taxation revenue.

UBS is a radical social and environmental strategy that could have wide appeal. Each city, region, or country has distinct levels of dilapidated or unavailable infrastructure and public resources—from parks or lack of health care to threatened ecosystems—and hence needs specifically formulated transitional strategies. These could be provided initially through a combination of free goods and services and more local public providers, rather than existing costly but profitable public-private enterprise contracts. The development of social wage essentials for workers and families could be planned in conjunction with phased reductions in per capita and national use of material resources. Rather than piece-meal welfare incrementalism offered by centre-Left parties during elections, a UBS strategy could facilitate public participation in local, regional, and national planning targets to maximise essential services and help the transition to a more caring and sustainable world. In contrast to utopian techno-fixes such as 'fully automated luxury communism' that are environmentally unsustainable, a UBS requires no science-fiction technology or unlimited fiscal resources. It is ready to be implemented now, if only the political will and sufficient popular support were forthcoming.

References

Bastani, Aaron. 2019. *Fully Automated Luxury Communism: A Manifesto*. London: Verso.

Bentham, J., Andrew Bowman, Marta de la Cuesta, Ewald Engelen, Ismail Ertürk, Peter Folkman, Julie Froud, Suhkdev Johal, John Law, Adam Leaver, Michael Moran, and Karl Williams. 2013. *Manifesto for the Foundational Economy*. Manchester: Centre for Research on Socio-Cultural Change, CRESC Working Paper No. 131.

Coote, Anna, Pritika Kasliwal, and Andrew Percy. 2019. *Universal Basic Services, Theory and Practice: A Literature Review*. London: UCL Institute for Global Prosperity.

Frankel, Boris. 2018. *Fictions of Sustainability: The Politics of Growth and Post-Capitalist Futures*. Melbourne: Greenmeadows.

———. 2020. *Capitalism Versus Democracy? Rethinking Politics in the Age of Environmental Crisis*. Melbourne: Greenmeadows.

Frase, Peter, Angela Nagle, Leigh Phillips, Michael Rozworski, and Christian Parenti. 2017. *Earth, Wind, and Fire*. Special Issue of *Jacobin*, no. 26.

Hall, Stephen, and Alex Schafran. 2017. From Foundational Economics and the Grounded City to Foundational Urban Systems. *Foundational Economy*, Working Paper No. 3.

Mason, Paul. 2015. *PostCapitalism: A Guide to Our Future*. London: Allen Lane.

Parrique, Timothée, Jonathan Barth, Francois Briens, Christian Kerschner, Alejo Kraus-Polk, Anna Kuokkanen, and Joachim Spangenberg. 2019. *Decoupling Debunked: Evidence and Arguments Against Green Growth as a Sole Strategy for Sustainability*. European Environment Bureau, July.

Rifkin, Jeremy. 2014. *The Zero Marginal Cost Society: The Internet of Things, the Collaborative Commons, and the Eclipse of Capitalism*. London: Palgrave Macmillan.

Social Prosperity Network. 2017. *Social Prosperity for the Future: A Proposal for Universal Basic Services*. London: Institute for Global Prosperity, UCL.

Srnicek, Nick, and Alex Williams. 2016. *Inventing the Future: Postcapitalism and a World Without Work*, revised and updated edition. London: Verso.

Vadén, Tere, Ville Lähde, Antti Majava, Paavo Järvensivu, Tero Toivanen, Emma Hakala, and Jussi Eronen. 2020. Decoupling for Ecological Sustainability: A Categorisation and Review of Research Literature. *Environmental Science and Policy* 112: 236–244.

8

Ecofeminist Political Economy: Critical Reflections on the Green New Deal

Christine Bauhardt

Ever since the US Congress's February 2019 resolution initiated by Alexandria Ocasio Cortez, the Green New Deal has been discussed widely, at least in the US and Europe. In December 2019 the European Union also announced a major investment programme called 'European Green Deal' with the goal of reaching zero emissions of greenhouse gases by 2050. Most CO_2 emissions due to carbon combustion are to be avoided; a smaller part of the carbon is to be stored. It is common knowledge that the concept of the Green New Deal harks back to Franklin D. Roosevelt's policy programme from the 1930s which aimed to boost growth and employment after the Great Depression by means of government investments in public infrastructure. Accordingly, Ursula von der Leyen, President of the European Commission, also considers her 'environmental pact' to be a strategy for economic growth: 'The European Green Deal is our new growth strategy,' she said when presenting her plan for the conversion of industry, technologies, and the financial system.

C. Bauhardt (✉)
Humboldt University of Berlin, Berlin, Germany
e-mail: christine.bauhardt@gender.hu-berlin.de

The United Kingdom put the concept on the agenda as early as 2007, when Caroline Lucas, at the time the only British Member of the European Parliament for the Greens, and others established the Green New Deal Group during the financial crisis. Arguing for a Green New Deal in the UK here and now, she wrote in the *Financial Times* in the summer of 2019: 'What was needed then—and is needed even more now—is a huge investment in renewable energy and energy efficiency programmes to insulate every building in Britain, a move to a more sustainable farming system, and to bring hope and jobs to communities hollowed out by deindustrialisation.' (Lucas 2019).

This brief quote highlights the perspective of the Green New Deal which has long been criticised by feminists (cf. Kuhl and Maier 2012; Bauhardt 2014): narrowing the socio-ecological transformation of society to technical innovations and mostly male-dominated sectors, disregarding the underpaid and unpaid care labour performed mostly by women. A Green New Deal is to make public investments in the policy fields of energy, mobility, and building more energy efficient, and in the best case bring about energy savings. Carbon-based fossil fuels are to be replaced by renewables, thus making lifestyles and consumption patterns more sustainable. The idea is that the investments in these areas will generate a large number of new jobs in innovative sectors of the economy. Less innovative, but nonetheless key for discontinuing carbon-based production methods, is the agricultural sector with its high consumption of energy for cultivation, irrigation, and transportation, as well as petroleum-based fertilisers.

The first chapter in Jeremy Rifkin's most recent book is titled 'It's the Infrastructure, Stupid!' (Rifkin 2019), and it refers solely to technical infrastructures: wind and solar energy for power generation, novel ways of powering vehicles and the expansion of rail services to secure mobility, and improved information and communication technologies to manage and optimise them. It is astonishing how little thought is given to the fact that these areas concern mostly male-dominated jobs, and they are very strongly associated with masculinity in symbolic terms as well (cf. Siemiatycki et al. 2019). The most striking feature is the linkage of technical performance with certain images of masculinity—courageous inventions, control over nature, and competence in dealing with technical artefacts. But this does not bring people to think critically about what image this 'bold economic plan to save life on Earth'—the muscular subtitle Jeremy Rifkin chose for his book—actually paints. In my mind's eye, it conjures up pictures of pit workers going down into the mines and sweating rail workers toiling to build the great railway systems, except that the dauntless engineers are now wearing suits and their fingernails aren't dirty anymore.

What would be the features of an economy that both recognises that the natural resources are finite and also accommodates feminist calls for more gender justice? Would it suffice to demand more jobs for women in tech, for example, by promoting women in the Science, Technology, Engineering, and Mathematics (STEM) fields? The ecofeminist discussion answers these questions with a clear no. Instead, it raises other questions: which competencies, which kinds of work does a society need to meet human needs? What are the foundations of life and the economy without which a society cannot exist? Neither the market alone nor technical innovations can satisfy needs. Instead, needs are met by women, often invisibly, in the so-called private realm of social reproduction, through generative reproduction as well as shouldering the work of everyday caring and taking responsibility for people who are not yet or are no longer capable of taking care of themselves (cf. as an overview: Bauhardt 2019). Women also bear the burden of a great deal of menial labour in the public sphere, whether it be in agriculture, cleaning, textiles and clothing manufacturing, high-tech component manufacturing, etc.

Ecofeminist Political Economy of Capitalism

Following contemporary analyses of the crises of capitalism—the crisis of overproduction, the banking crisis, the environmental crisis—current voices in feminist economics speak of the crisis of social reproduction. Feminist economists use the term to denote the under-provision of care, which is above all time-consuming and inaccessible to the rationalisation efforts of the capitalist mode of production—and which in principle should not be accessible to rationalisation because of the nature of the reproductive work. Social reproduction work is performed both without pay in private households and—usually for little pay—via the labour market (including cash-in-hand work). Important characteristics of this work include that it cannot be postponed and that it requires interpersonal empathy and high levels of reliability and commitment. The 'crisis of social reproduction' indicates that the expansion of the capitalist logic of exploitation also reshapes care labour through the economic imperative of acceleration, rationalisation, and intensification of work.

Both sides, those providing and those receiving care, perceive the crisis of social reproduction in the overwork and the excessive demands placed on those people responsible for care labour. Under the prevailing circumstances of the gender-hierarchical division of labour, the vast majority of caregivers are women: women perform by far the greatest share of unpaid familial labour, not only caring for children, but also ensuring that males' labour is available to the labour market, even though the women are gainfully employed themselves. It is also women who take on most of the social reproduction occurring in the sphere of paid labour, be it in raising and teaching children or caring for the sick and the elderly. An often-used way out of being overburdened because of the crisis in care is delegating reproductive labour in one's own household to migrant women or racialised women—also known as the 'global care chain' (Salazar Parreñas 2015). This is a clear sign of the fact that despite a long-standing debate about the gendered division of labour, men have not taken on their share of unpaid work in everyday care labour.

Feminist economists of different schools of thought agree that it is key for the feminist analysis of capitalism to view social reproduction as a realm that is (at least) equivalent to and just as relevant in economic terms as market-based 'productive gainful employment'—productive because it produces goods and surplus value. From the perspective of the economy overall, investments in social infrastructure—that is, education, care, nursing, etc.—are considered to be consumption expenditure, and unpaid work in private households, to the extent it is viewed as work at all, is considered to be re-productive. These terms and concepts and the premises they involve are the subject of a lively debate among feminists, which I will go into briefly.

The concept of re-production was already contradicted by feminists early on: why should only the manufacture of goods for exchange be considered 'productive', but not the 'manufacture' of life and the maintenance of living processes? On further consideration: why is only the processing of nature considered productive, but not nature as such? These questions are the starting point for ecofeminist analysis of the relationships of society to nature under capitalism. This links the ecological criticism of the exploitation and overuse of natural resources with the feminist criticism of the exploitation and societal appropriation of the (unpaid or underpaid) work performed by women in social reproduction (Mellor 1997).

This work is invisible economically, and for this reason it is grossly underestimated because it is work performed by women, which puts it in proximity to nature: because of their potential ability to give birth, women are assumed to be predestined as if 'by nature' to care for people who cannot care for themselves. In other words: it is assumed that women are born with competencies for care 'by nature' and that they do not need to learn and develop them and thus do not need to be paid. Such competencies are taken for granted—and in fact no society, whether capitalist or not, could survive without women's social reproduction labour. So, from an ecofeminist perspective, the relationships of society to nature under capitalism are characterised by dual power relations: by subordination and exploitation of nature and of women's labour which has been declared socially and historically part of nature.

Thus, strategies for an environmentally sound and socially just transition to a post-capitalist era must consider the gendered power relations in human–nature relationships: 'Central to feminist ecological economics is the normative claim that gender equality should not be achieved at the expense of ecological degradation or the exploitation of nature and other species and that environmental sustainability must not be achieved by exploiting feminised labour' (Cohen and MacGregor 2020: 8).

The entire economic sector of the care economy, which includes both paid and unpaid labour, is still disregarded in the debates around the Green New Deal. If the care sector were also discussed under the guiding principle of 'public investments in infrastructure policy', then the debate would have to be conducted in a completely different way. After all, the expansion of the care infrastructure would also imply a fundamental change in how the economy is organised in a post-fossil society. There would be a commensurate focus on the overexploitation of women's labour as the overexploitation of the fossil resources. The creation of jobs in social infrastructure would provide secure livelihoods for women and create new ones—for all genders!—and the labour *conditions* in these occupations would have to be discussed.

Ecofeminist Political Economy of the Green New Deal

But what would happen with the unpaid care work in the so-called private households? This is the fundamental weakness of the Green New Deal: it focuses on the public sector of economic activity; the private sphere of people's 'own four walls' and the work performed there are still disregarded, as in the traditional economic debates and theories. So far, the fact that the participation of women in the paid labour markets of industrialised societies has constantly increased in recent years has not resulted in men and women sharing unpaid housework. Since this work must be done, however, private housework and care work have been shifted within middle-class households to migrant women workers. This has been described as the 'global care chain' and is discussed critically from a feminist perspective. From an intersectional perspective of dividing care work into paid and unpaid sectors of economic activity, the Green New Deal is to be viewed especially critically because it is limited to the public realm and leaves the power relations in the private sphere untouched.

The ecofeminist view takes the totality of economic activities for satisfying human needs into account, regardless of whether they are paid or unpaid and whether they are organised in the public or private realms. This permits us to perceive other ways to meet these needs. This perspective also changes the line of vision to be taken by a Green New Deal: departing from the technical-technocratic focus and adopting a way of life and production that does more justice to human beings and most probably also to nature.

What would this mean for the concept of the Green New Deal? The infrastructure policy at the centre of the debate must encompass technical infrastructures as well as social ones. They function according to different logics and follow different ethical orientations. The logic of technical infrastructures is that of rationalisation, acceleration, and subordination of nature. Its orientation is not normative-ethical, but rather functionalist. There is no need to call these logics and orientations 'masculine', but they do have some androcentric substance in the sense that they disregard or are wilfully blind to the modes of social reproduction that underpins them.

The social infrastructures for educating children and caring for them and for people who are sick temporarily or long term, or who are old or need long-term care, follow different logics and normative orientations—or at least they should if the work performed there is to be successful. It is the logic and the ethics of care that drive action here, where it is about living beings and not about technical artefacts, where time prosperity is needed instead of acceleration, and where the natural rhythms of growing, becoming, and passing away determine the general course of action. This logic is not necessarily 'feminine', either, but seems to reproduce itself time and again following the symbolic order and hierarchy of the gender binary.

Ecofeminist Political Economy Beyond Green Growth

One fundamental problem of the Green New Deal is yet to be discussed. This policy approach is a strategy to promote economic growth, as emphasised by the President of the European Commission, who was quoted at the beginning of this piece: the Green New Deal promotes infrastructures for green growth. This means that it does not question the growth imperative of the capitalist economic order. Indeed, growth is seen as the panacea for the latest iteration of capitalist crisis.

Infrastructure policy seeks to incentivise or develop inputs for capital accumulation that capital is neither willing nor able to provide.

Infrastructures are essential for capitalist societies to function. They are considered the foundation of an economy based on the division of labour: such a foundation is a prerequisite for the production, distribution, and use of goods and services. They are basic material and institutional structures that underpin all economic processes of the valorisation of capital. Making high-performance infrastructures available requires large investments which individual capital is unable to make—and is unwilling to make, since the expected returns cannot be calculated short term or returns cannot be expected in the first place—or benefits are collective rather than individual creating 'free rider' concerns for capital. Technical and social infrastructures are characterised by various elements of collectivity. They are financed collectively through the tax system, they require a high degree of collective planning and coordination if they are to fulfil their purpose, and in principle they are available for all to use.

Highly differentiated societies rely on the institutional and material organisation of the division of labour, so it would not be expedient to work politically towards abolishing infrastructure policy. The question arises whether it is possible to imagine an infrastructure policy that is not oriented towards economic growth, but towards sustaining, repairing, and renewing what already exists. In other words, a Green New Deal that neither encourages more of the same capitalist logic of exploitation nor pursues romanticised notions of a pre-industrial and pre-modern world.

Accordingly, my ideas for a Green New Deal with an intersectional and gender-equitable orientation would have to take the needs of social reproduction as their starting point and develop the logics of infrastructure policy following the ethical-normative orientations of social reproduction. The dichotomisation of androcentric-functionalist rationality in the development of technology on the one hand and a care ethic that is implicitly identified as 'feminine' on the other must be overcome by an infrastructure policy that places the needs of human beings and their reproductive needs at the centre of its deliberations—without additional and damaging resource consumption and destruction of the ecological foundations of life. Global gender justice and environmental justice do not contradict each other, but rather complement one another if they are conceived of as one.

References

Bauhardt, Christine. 2014. 'Solutions to the Crisis? The Green New Deal, Degrowth, and the Solidarity Economy: Alternatives to the Capitalist Growth Economy from an Ecofeminist Economics Perspective. *Ecological Economics* 102: 60–68.

———. 2019. Nature, Care and Gender: Feminist Dilemmas. In *Feminist Political Ecology and the Economics of Care: In Search of Economic Alternatives*, Routledge Studies in Ecological Economics, ed. Christine Bauhardt and Wendy Harcourt, 16–35. London: Routledge.

Cohen, Maeve, and Sherilyn MacGregor. 2020. Towards a Feminist Green New Deal for the UK. A Paper for the WBG Commission on A Gender-Equal Economy. Accessed 12 August 2020. www.wbg.org.uk.

Kuhl, Mara, in cooperation with Friederike Maier. 2012. The Gender Dimensions of the Green New Deal—An Analysis of Policy Papers of the Greens/EFA New Deal Working Group. Berlin. (Study commissioned by The Greens/EFA Group in the European Parliament, initiated by Elisabeth Schroedter).

Lucas, Caroline. 2019. Britain Needs Its Own Green New Deal: The Country Could be a World Leader in the Clean Energy Revolution. *Financial Times*, 8 June 2019.

Mellor, Mary. 1997. *Feminism & Ecology*. New York: New York University Press.

Rifkin, Jeremy. 2019. *The Green New Deal: Why the Fossil Fuel Civilization Will Collapse By 2028, and the Bold Economic Plan to Save Life on Earth*. New York: St Martin's Press.

Salazar Parreñas, Rhacel. 2015. *Servants of Globalization: Migration and Domestic Work*. Stanford: Stanford University Press.

Siemiatycki, Matti, Theresa Enright, and Mariana Valverde. 2019. The Gendered Production of Infrastructure. *Progress in Human Geography* 44 (2): 297–314.

The Green New Deal Group. n.d. Accessed 12 August 2020. https://greennewdealgroup.org/.

9

The Macroeconomics of Degrowth: Can Planned Economic Contraction Be Stable?

Steve Keen

The *Limits to Growth* is infamous for its 'Standard Run' scenario (Meadows et al. 1972, Figure 35: 124), which predicted that, if there were no changes to the direction of economic development after 1972, then by some time in the early to mid-twenty-first century, human civilisation would undergo a serious decline.

Less well known is its 'Stabilised Run', in which a range of policies were hypothetically introduced in 1975 to achieve a state of 'global equilibrium … so that the basic material needs of each person on earth are satisfied' (Meadows et al. 1972: 24). The simulation concluded that no single policy was sufficient, but if all the policies they modelled were undertaken, the world could achieve a sustainable future where average living standards for the globe were three times as high as they were in 1970, and much more equitably distributed.

As crucial as the need for a swathe of policies was the timing: if the changes were delayed until 2000, then they would fail, there would be

S. Keen (✉)
Institute for Strategy, Resilience and Security, University College London, London, UK

overshoot of the biosphere's capability to endure the pressure put upon it by humanity's industrialised society. Both output and population would reach a peak in the mid-twenty-first century and then decline.

It is stating the obvious that policies to restrain humanity's pressure on the biosphere were not put in place in 1975, nor 2000, nor even 2020. With research by Graham Turner (Turner 2008; Turner et al. 2011; Turner 2014) confirming that the world is still largely tracking the Standard Run of *Limits to Growth*, and studies like the 'Ecological Footprint' (Global Footprint Network 2018) asserting that the human species alone is using 1.7 times the reproducible limit of the biosphere, we are well into ecological overshoot.

Meadows et al. noted that there were only two possibilities for the future: 'a self-imposed limitation to growth, or a nature-imposed limitation to growth' (Meadows et al. 1972: 168). Since we have clearly failed to impose limits ourselves, we now face Nature doing that for us.

Meadows et al. deliberately avoided providing precise timing for their predictions (Meadows et al. 1972: 123–124), but it is hardly being hyperbolic, at this point in 2020, to feel that the deliberately vague timing of the *Limits to Growth* has proven to be precisely correct. Nature is imposing its limits now.

Just as COVID-19 has led to policy changes that were unthinkable as recently as January 2020, what if it and subsequent ecological calamities shook humanity so much that we decided, belatedly but instantly, to impose the limits that *Limits to Growth* recommended we should implement 45 years ago? What would happen to global GDP?

Answering this question thoroughly would require an updated *Limits to Growth*. That this does not exist is due in large measure to the ferocious attacks on its credibility by economists in general, and William Nordhaus in particular (Nordhaus 1973, 1992). These attacks, based on misinformation and ignorance rather than knowledge (Forrester et al. 1974; Keen 2020a), had devastating consequences. Though the book sold millions of copies, the group's research funding evaporated. Whereas the original study was run on state-of-the-art mainframe computers with a million-dollar budget in 1972, today Jorgen Randers is working without pay on developing an extended version called MODCAP, using the PC-based system dynamics program Vensim.

However, in lieu of a complete answer, a partial one can be provided by focusing on one of the many weaknesses of economics: the failure to properly acknowledge the essential role of energy in production. What will happen to GDP if humanity realises that it must immediately cease adding CO_2 to the atmosphere, by ceasing to use carbon-based forms of energy, for everything from the production of electricity to transportation?

This question cannot be answered by economic models, since they treat GDP as being generated by a combination of labour and capital alone: Labour and machinery in, goods and services out. But neither workers nor machines can function without energy. As we put it in 'A Note on the Role of Energy in Production' (Keen et al. 2019: 41): 'Labour without energy is a corpse; capital without energy is a sculpture.' If there is no energy input, then there is no GDP, and if energy inputs fall, then *ipso facto*, so will GDP.

This could be countered if there were a trend for GDP to 'decouple' from energy, so that more GDP could be produced per unit of energy, and if there were also a strong trend for non-carbon-based forms of energy to replace fossil fuels, so that the overall fall in energy could be attenuated. Both these counters are false hopes. Though there has been a trend to a falling level of energy per unit of GDP in some countries, at the global level, the relationship between energy consumption and GDP between 1971 and 2017 is extremely tight: see Fig. 9.1. A rising global GDP requires a rising level of energy, and since energy is the motive force, if we are forced to abandon carbon-based energy forms, GDP has to fall by much the same fraction as carbon-based energy is of total energy.

The remaining hope is that progress in renewable energy has been such that it makes up a much larger proportion of total energy production than in the past. But again, data dashes hope: though there has been a rapid increase in renewable energy as a percentage of total energy production since 2007, non-carbon-based energy (including nuclear and hydro) still constitute just 18.7 per cent of total energy output in 2020 (IEA 2020). Shutting down carbon-based fuels now would cause GDP to fall by the order of 80 per cent.

But what if the wildfires, and the virus, and the floods, and the locusts(!) of 2020 are followed by other ecological nightmares that finally alert humanity to how far we have overstepped the carrying capacity of this

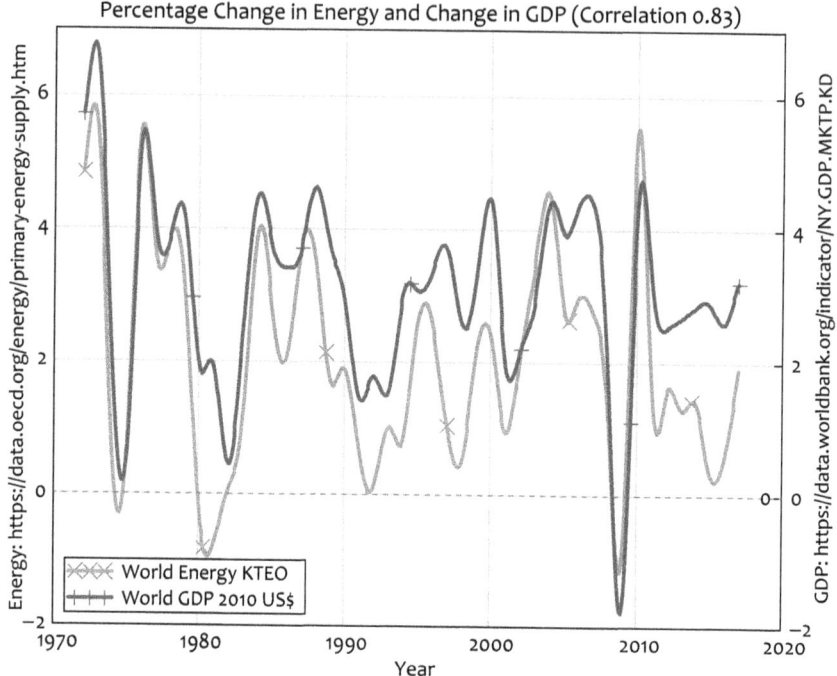

Fig. 9.1 The relationship between change in energy and change in GDP

planet, and policymakers, with support from the public, adopt the UK Labour target of 2030 as the year in which CO_2 emissions fall to zero Jackson (2019)? Given the almost linear relationship between energy usage and GDP, what would it take to preserve 2020's global real output level in 2030?

With an estimated pre-COVID-19 global GDP in 2020 of $86 trillion (in 2010 US$ terms), and energy production of 14 million KTOE (KiloTonnes of Oil Equivalent), to reach 100 per cent renewable energy by 2030, starting from 18 per cent in 2020, would require the installation of roughly four large (1000 Megawatt) solar/wind/hydro-electric, or nuclear power stations every day, for a decade. It goes without saying that we do not have the capacity to achieve this goal.

This means that we won't be able to maintain 2020 GDP levels in 2030 with an economy that has net zero CO_2 emissions. Though we should still endeavour to expand non-carbon-based power as much as possible, if we are to have a zero-carbon economy by 2030, then we have to accept that GDP will fall substantially. Even a fourfold increase in the rate of growth of renewable energy will result in energy input levels—and hence GDP output levels—that are 50 per cent below 2020 levels in 2030.

How could such a reduction in output be undertaken deliberately and, as much as possible, peacefully? We need a mechanism for GDP reduction, and for the encouragement of the shift to renewable energy, that falls primarily on the wealthy. A price for carbon, as championed by Neoclassical economists like William Nordhaus, will afflict the poor disproportionately compared to the rich. The riots with which the Gilets Jaunes movement began in France (in October 2018) in response to carbon pricing should make it obvious that the burden of adjustment must fall on the rich rather than the poor—both within nations and between them.

One feasible mechanism is a modification of Fleming's *Tradeable Energy Quota* (TEQ) proposal (Fleming and Chamberlin 2011; Fleming 2016), which puts the burden of adjustment firmly on the wealthy: a dual-price mechanism, as proposed by Total Carbon Rationing. Tradeable Universal Carbon Credits (UCCs) would be distributed via Central Bank Digital Currencies (CBDCs) to every resident on an equal per capita basis—so that billionaires would receive the same annual UCC as paupers. To buy any commodity, a consumer would need to pay both its money price, as now, and its CO_2 content as well, using UCCs.

The ration would initially be set above the average per capita CO_2 consumption of each country, so that the vast majority of the population would not exhaust their allowance and would therefore be able to sell their excess UCCs to the rich—who, at their current consumption levels, would definitely exhaust their allowance, and thus need to buy UCCs from the poor. It would work as a redistributive mechanism, as well as a means to reduce consumption and hence GDP and CO_2 output. The ration could be reduced over time, as with Fleming's TEQs proposal.

Any degrowth economic regime must also confront the remnants of its growth-obsessed predecessor. The 2008 crisis was driven by a private debt and credit bubble, and its botched aftermath has resulted in a

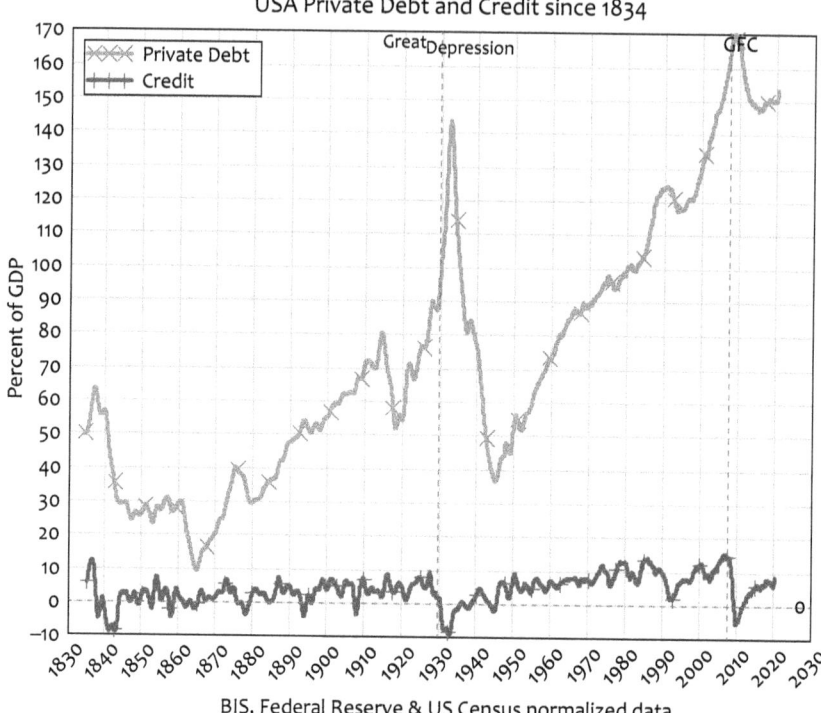

Fig. 9.2 The 2008 crisis left the USA and the world with the highest private debt levels in history

private debt level that still exceeds the peak of the Great Depression (see Fig. 9.2).

Ignoring this debt overhang in a degrowth world could lead to a financial disaster, even if UCCs placed the burden of adjustment primarily on the wealthy. It is highly unlikely that business in the aggregate will be profitable in a degrowth world, especially in one where, since we have failed to take action for so long, the decline in GDP must be that much steeper than *Limits to Growth* envisioned. Without both a dramatic reduction in outstanding private debt, and a supplementary cash flow to enable corporate and household financial commitments to be met as the physical economy contracts, the financial system could collapse and bring the physical adjustment process to a chaotic halt. Two mechanisms could avoid this fate: a Modern Debt Jubilee (Steve Keen 2017: 117–121) and a Universal Basic Income (UBI) (see Chap. 2 of this volume).

Both can be financed simply by the government creating the necessary money. As both Modern Monetary Theory (Kelton 2020) and the practice of quantitative easing (Coppola 2019) have shown, a currency-issuing government can create as much money as it wishes—the constraints are the effects of such money creation, rather than its feasibility. There is no possibility of a currency-issuing government running out of its own currency.

Nor is there any chance of a domestic-currency-denominated bond sale not being fully subscribed. Though sales of Treasury bonds give the appearance that a government deficit is financed by borrowing from private banks, in fact the deficit itself creates both money in private sector bank accounts on the liability side of the banking sector's ledger, and excess reserves on the asset side. Bond sales then enable banks to undertake a favourable asset swap, exchanging non-interest-earning reserves for interest-earning Treasury bonds. A failure of the finance sector to buy all Treasury bonds on issue would be a failure to be greedy, which is something we can safely assume won't happen.

A Modern Debt Jubilee would issue government-fiat-created money to all residents on a per-capita basis. Those with debt would be required to pay their debt down. Those without debt would be required to buy newly issued corporate shares, which corporations would be required to use to pay down corporate debt. This could eliminate the private debt overhang, and democratise the ownership of corporations at the same time.

State payments to individuals during the COVID-19 crisis have also shown that a UBI is practical—again, with the government deficit creating the money required to finance it. This would enable a country's residents to buy the necessarily basic commodities needed to survive during a sustained period of degrowth—though the problem of whether those commodities could actually be manufactured would become more acute as degrowth continued. This is clearly more a monetary command economy than a capitalist market economy, but such will be necessary to survive the crisis that a period of unconstrained market-oriented growth has given us.

An economically, financially, and politically stable route to reduced GDP is thus conceivable. But is it realistic? My expectation is that it is not. Though these policies would make survival of human society more likely, they would come at the expense of the power of the financial elite of current-day society. The far more likely outcome is that humanity in general and the powerful in particular will delay the decision to act, hoping instead that GDP can return to pre-COVID-19 growth rates, while ignoring the dependence of this growth rate on an increasing use of carbon-based energy that will accelerate global warming.

These policies will also become necessary at a time of multiple crises that will increase social conflict, making initiatives like this harder to implement. We are witnessing this already. The US has been humbled by the coronavirus, and divided by President Trump's inept and malicious response to it. As I write these words (September 2020), this singular tragedy is being amplified in the drought-stricken state of California by storms that created both the first ever fire tornadoes and a 'lightning siege' of 11,000 bolts over a single weekend that sparked 367 wildfires (Fuller 2020). California's capacity to respond to any one of these crises is diminished by the others: evacuees from fires cannot be housed in dormitories for fear of spreading COVID-19; the prisoner fire crews that normally fight such fires have been halved by the coronavirus itself. Crises like these do not add to each other but multiply each other.

While we squabble, Nature will make the final decision for us.

References

Coppola, Frances. 2019. *People's Quantitative Easing*. Cambridge: Polity Press.
Fleming, David. 2016. *Lean Logic: A Dictionary for the Future and How to Survive It*. London: Chelsea Green.
Fleming, David, and Sean Chamberlin. 2011. *TEQs: Tradable Energy Quotas: A Policy Framework for Peak Oil and Climate Change*. London: House of Commons All Party Parliamentary Group on Peak Oil & The Lean Economy Connection.
Forrester, Jay Wright, W. Low Gilbert, et al. 1974. The Debate on "World Dynamics": A Response to Nordhaus. *Policy Sciences* 5 (2): 169–190.
Fuller, Thomas. 2020. Fires, Blackouts, a Heat Wave and a Pandemic: California's "Horrible" Month. *The New York Times* (19 August 2020).

Global Footprint Network. 2018. Data and Methodology. Accessed 5 December 2020. https://www.footprintnetwork.org/resources/data/

International Energy Agency (IEA). 2020. *Key World Energy Statistics 2020*. Paris: International Energy Agency.

Jackson, Tim. 2019. Carbon Zero Sooner: The Case for an Early Zero Carbon Target for the UK. CUSP Working Paper. Accessed 15 August 2020. https://www.cusp.ac.uk/themes/aetw/zero-carbon-sooner/

Keen, Steve. 2017. *Can We Avoid Another Financial Crisis? (the Future of Capitalism)*. London: Polity Press.

———. 2020a. The Appallingly Bad Neoclassical Economics of Climate Change. *Globalizations*. Accessed 5 December 2020. https://doi.org/10.1080/14747731.2020.1807856

———. 2020b. Emergent Macroeconomics: Deriving Minsky's Financial Instability Hypothesis Directly from Macroeconomic Definitions. *Review of Political Economy* 32 (2): 342–370.

Keen, Steve, Robert U. Ayres, et al. 2019. A Note on the Role of Energy in Production. *Ecological Economics* 157: 40–46.

Kelton, Stephanie. 2020. *The Deficit Myth: Modern Monetary Theory and the Birth of the People's Economy*. New York: Public Affairs.

Meadows, Donnella, Jorgen Randers, et al. 1972. *The Limits to Growth*. New York: Signet.

Nordhaus, William. 1973. World Dynamics: Measurement Without Data. *The Economic Journal* 83 (332): 1156–1183.

———. 1992. Lethal Model 2: The Limits to Growth Revisited. *Brookings Papers on Economic Activity* 2: 1–43.

Turner, Graham. 2008. A Comparison of The Limits to Growth with 30 Years of Reality. *Global Environmental Change* 18 (3): 397–411.

———. 2014. *Is Global Collapse Imminent? An Updated Comparison of The Limits to Growth with Historical Data*. Melbourne: Melbourne Sustainable Society Institute, University of Melbourne.

Turner, Graham, Robert Hoffman, et al. 2011. A Tool for Strategic Biophysical Assessment of a National Economy—The Australian Stocks and Flows Framework. *Environmental Modelling & Software* 26: 1134–1149.

10

Post-Capitalist Techno-Futures: Beyond Instrumental Utopianism

Sangeetha Chandrashekeran and Jathan Sadowski

As socio-environmental crises intensify, a growing number of billionaires, in the upper echelons of technology and finance, have volunteered themselves as the world's saviours. As the grave state of ecological disrepair and social injustice become more evident to the global elites and harder to deny, they dig deeper into their bag of technofix tricks and see opportunity emerging out of crisis. Bill Gates, for example, offered one solution for how to combat climate change: 'We need hundreds of Elon Musks and that's how we'll get this done' (Yilek 2021: np). Meanwhile, Larry Fink, the CEO of BlackRock, the world's largest asset manager, declared in his 2021 'Letter to CEOs' that now is the time to begin the 'transition to a net zero economy' by 2050—while his company maintains massive investments in the fossil fuel industry (in addition to nearly every other

---

S. Chandrashekeran (✉)
Melbourne Sustainable Society Institute, University of Melbourne, Parkville, VIC, Australia
e-mail: sangeetha.chandra@unimelb.edu.au

J. Sadowski
Monash University, Clayton, VIC, Australia

sector) (Fink 2021). These paragons of capitalism see their superior position in society—not to mention their record-breaking profits in the midst of a global pandemic—as evidence that only they possess the leadership and innovation to confront the next waves of crises crashing down on us all. They have worked hard to assert their dominion over the world, so why not the future, too? Now is the time for utopian thinking, but only, according to the Gateses, Musks, and Finks of the world, if those utopias preserve their interests and (masculine) authority.

For decades, we have been largely trapped within the boundaries of techno-capitalist futurism.

Silicon Valley has established its sole ownership of the means of producing utopia. Yet rather than offer radical solutions for universal human liberation, their programmatic thinking instrumentalises utopianism, reducing it to a tool for manufacturing consent for tech companies' hegemony. By their formulation, there's only one pathway forward, one possible future. And the only way we'll get there is through technocratic governance, efficiency improvements, and 'smart' solutions, which they'll happily implement as long as they're given the reins—and nobody tries standing in their way.

It is important that we unsettle and challenge these narratives of technological triumphalism without succumbing to a 'back to nature' anti-tech reaction. We must re-embed techno-futurism, and our analysis of alternatives, in the realities of the workings of capital and its social relations. This involves revealing the operations of a system that 'seeks to subjugate the demands of the many to the desires of the few' (Sadowski 2021: np). But not stopping there. We need to go further and envision positive technological futures where appropriate technology is oriented first and foremost to basic provisioning for those most in need; where benefits are not filtered through a system of trickle-down innovation; where the means and abilities to make decisions about production aren't held by a small group of large hands, and where monopolistic concentrations of profit and power are regulated, rather than relied on to promote the public good.

Like good speculative fiction that observes the conditions of today to create projections of tomorrow, social science has an important role to play in unpacking the nature of contemporary problems and articulating positive futures that can then be visualised in a variety of ways. As critical scholars, we need to do more conjuring of post-capitalist futures, and do so in ways that are clear-eyed about the relations of power and domination of the current moment. Only then can we chart our way out of the crisis-ridden present into more hopeful futures. There is no ground zero from which we reorient our economy-society; we'd rather not reach a point where the world must be rebuilt from its ashes. Instead, we must harness the tools and labour we have to create something better out of the reality we find ourselves in.

In this chapter we use examples from the highly imperfect world we occupy to think through the fault lines and opportunities for a shift to more just and socially embedded technological futures. This involves understanding where the fissures and points of contradiction lie. From there we can chart an imagined path out of these that foregrounds the radical potential inherent in conjunctures. In the next section we discuss two relevant, ongoing movements—for worker power and for data sovereignty—that seek to challenge the hegemony of technology companies.

Working Against Big Tech

The dominant visions of techno-utopias deliberately obscure the underlying exploitation on which they are based—this includes 'smart' futures where digital platforms, using cutting-edge capabilities of data-driven, networked, and automated logistics, own and operate the essential services and infrastructure of everyday life (Sadowski 2020). For example, the successful vote for Proposition 22 in California in 2020 allowed gig economy companies like Uber and Lyft to classify drivers as independent contractors, thus allowing them to deny benefits to workers who are the functional equivalent of employees. This outcome further entrenches the exploitative labour practices of the gig economy: enshrining a sub-minimum-wage floor and the practice of remunerating only for designated activities, but not the time made available to undertake the activities.

The campaign against Proposition 22 led by non-union labour organisers like the Gig Workers Collective managed to build an impressive grassroots movement through a lot of time, energy, and small donations by volunteer activists. They sought to give the atomised workers on these platforms a collective voice, and they succeeded in raising more public awareness about the consequences of this ballot measure. But ultimately, their efforts were dwarfed by the US$205 million campaign in favour of Proposition 22 led by companies like Uber and Lyft, the largest amount ever spent campaigning for a state ballot measure. These companies, like the activists against them, saw Proposition 22 as a threshold vote with implications for policy and operations across the US and globally. The techno-utopia of on-demand service provision rests on companies' claims of providing flexibility for workers and lower prices for consumers. These are played off against the rights of workers for liveable wages and basic occupational health and safety protections.

Another example is the struggle of Amazon employees in Bessemer, Alabama, to be the first unionised warehouse ('fulfillment centre') in the United States. The Retail, Wholesale, and Department Store Union (RWDSU), a majority Black union representing a majority Black workforce in a majority Black city, has highlighted the inequitable distribution of Amazon's earnings back to workers. A vote to unionise the workforce has been hard fought against by Amazon, which fears a wave of union organising from its 400,000 warehouse employees across the country. Amazon has engaged in deliberate anti-union messaging and tactics, such as setting up an anti-union website, holding mandatory meetings for workers on company time decrying unionisation, and even getting the local government to change the timing on traffic lights near the warehouse to prevent organisers from talking to people coming in and out of the parking lot. This vote, which was ultimately unsuccessful for the union, was nonetheless the first ballot for unionisation by Amazon employees since 2014, and a historic battle given non-agricultural union membership has declined to just 11 per cent in 2020, in line with the demise of US manufacturing.

These two examples of workers' collective action re-embed the activities of platform capitalism in the fundamental relations of production. Digital platforms accelerate capital accumulation through processes of circulation and commodification and platform providers own the means of production. Companies like Uber and Amazon have successfully decoupled their share price from profit earnings. Despite consistently posting losses, they maintain the confidence of capital markets through their utopian predictions about the future, and aggressively fight actions that threaten the narrative of limitless exponential growth. Unlike in Europe, US labour laws only allow bargaining on a workplace—not sectoral—basis, putting workers in a structurally weak position against a global corporation. Despite the highly uneven playing field, an organised labour force at any scale is a fundamental 'disruption' to the visions of the tech sector, which is at the forefront of capitalist accumulation in the contemporary period.

Another important resistance front lies in active opposition to the acquisition of data by large tech firms. A core feature of living under a regime of digital capitalism is being enrolled in an ongoing and expanding process of data grabbing whereby our everyday activities are captured, linked, and analysed with a view to driving new innovations and accumulation opportunities. Data is commodified, its value inhering once again in future promises of ever greater returns on profit and power that usually involve greater automation and the enclosure of knowledge through patents. 'Data sovereignty', in the radical sense, involves actions by civil society or economic cooperatives to hold data in common as opposed to private ownership by big tech; to destroy rather than analyse for purposes of creating market value; and to store rather than export data (Fraser 2019). This is not an anti-tech position, rather it is an act of rebalancing technological visions away from the market-oriented claims of convenience and flexibility at all costs towards reshaping technological architectures in line with principles of economic and social justice and underlying class relations.

There are numerous examples worldwide of data sovereignty initiatives. We highlight here the work of a US cooperative of agriculture producers who have created a data storage repository controlled by growers themselves. AgXchange is an independent farmer-owned data repository that allows producers to control, store, view, and share their farm data assets on their own terms. Data is held in common rather than enclosed and privatised. For another example, we can also look to the city government in Barcelona, which has been working to reorient smart city systems away from their previously neoliberal arrangements, in partnership with the multinational firm Cisco, towards progressive policies and digital platforms that enhance participatory democracy and public ownership of data (Morozov and Bria 2018). Capitalist privatisation and market rule is resisted by promoting public governance and participatory governance for the common good. Alongside these shifts is a growing grassroots movement focused on claiming 'technological sovereignty', which aims to put into practice 'ways of imagining and building alternatives to the hegemonic model of technological development' (Lynch 2020: 10).

Principles for Post-Capitalist Techno-Politics

We see the pathway to post-capitalist technological futures emerging out of the transformation in the ownership of the means of production. What then could liberatory technological futures look like? Rather than prescribe a vision, we briefly outline key principles that ought to guide these visions and that deserve further attention, recognising that their form and content will need to be designed bottom-up not top-down, and will emerge out of the spatially specific struggles for justice and equity. These principles are Democratic Governance, Worker Power, Socially Beneficial Production, and Meaningful Labour.

Democratic governance involves data being conceived as a public good. It is more than a simplistic call for more open-source data to hold governments to account and solve 'wicked problems'. Rather it is about how connective capacity is leveraged for a collective purpose and radical social movements. The rhizomatic communication that the internet enables has been harnessed by white extremists and others to perpetuate old forms of violence in new ways. Therefore, any notion of democratic governance has to be accompanied by frameworks for accountability. This involves critical and direct engagement with processes of how data is created, who has the power to control and deploy it, and participation in devising radical alternatives. We need to look deep 'in the stack', to the layers of components and services that comprise software and applications, to understand how infrastructural decisions produce action, this includes terms of service, the architecture of virtual objects, how banal things like protocols encode the world and instantiate principles through techniques like scoring and distributing resources.

Accountability means rethinking the basic geometries of power institutionalised through monopolistic firms and deregulated markets—dominant features of capitalist economies—that are unburdened by public oversight, and governing through public accountability frameworks the companies that build the infrastructures of the internet that surround us. For example, when algorithmic decision-making results in discriminatory and inequitable outcomes we need standards of fairness and transparency to be enforced. This of course raises questions about where the locus of control lies, in whose interest are algorithms framed, and what happens when autonomous systems take the initial logic to new unseen places? Who are the computer scientists and engineers that create autonomous cyberphysical systems, and who gets a seat at the table to set standards and regulate them? These are all important matters of concern for a post-capitalist future that must be addressed in tandem with or in advance of the development of technology.

Worker power will begin with but eventually transcend the shopfloor struggles for better wages and conditions. There are stark asymmetries in the resources and capabilities of labour and capital. While the latter seeks representation in the market, the former exerts domination over the market. For labour movements to be successful in their fight for power, they must also be equipped with stronger political and social support. In terms of policy, antitrust actions have a key role to play in breaking the power blocs of technology capital and levelling the extraordinarily uneven market. It's far easier for labour movements to score wins against many smaller opponents versus mega-corporations with wealth and power that rival entire countries.

Additionally, technology capital has succeeded at pitting segments of the working class against each other such as when Uber threatened to pull its service out of California if they were forced to recognise their drivers as employees. Or, when companies like Amazon threaten to pass on the cost of better working conditions to consumers. By subsidising cheap and convenient services with labour exploitation and data extraction, technology capital creates an antagonistic relationship between users and workers. It's difficult to convince the public that worker power is a vital issue in society when the infrastructure of everyday life is now owned and operated by giant platform firms. For people to act collectively as citizens, rather than think individually as consumers, there must be publicly funded alternatives and stronger social services that help realign the interests of users and workers. A post-capitalist transition will, by necessity, have to be driven by organised labour in strong coalitions with other progressive voices.

All of this must be done in the service of subordinating technology development to the goal of **socially beneficial production and use**. In the 1970s Ivan Illich presciently made the case for the marginal disutility of tools, something that is understood implicitly by all of us who feel enslaved rather than empowered by technological acceleration and its plethora of complex options. He argued that after a certain point, more technological innovation gives negative returns, such that the gains for the most savvy and elite users correlates inversely to the equality and freedom of the vast majority of users. Society and community are eroded through the creation of hostile media landscapes which isolate and individualise, polarise and splinter the very qualities of community and connection that ironically features so heavily in tech advertising propaganda (Illich 1973). Illich calls for the development and deployment of *convivial* tools that are rooted in principles of equality, justice, fullness of meaning, and security and resilience. This vision sits in contrast with technological development under capitalism, which is shaped by the dictates of profit-maximisation, even if this comes at the expense of people and planet.

Key to socially beneficial technology development is the promotion of **meaningful production and labour**, instead of an economic order oriented around automation for accumulation, soul crushing jobs that keep us busy at all times, and promised relief in the form of endless convenience through market exchange. 'While corporations may engage in ruthless downsizing, the layoffs and speed-ups invariably fall on that class of people who are actually making, moving, fixing and maintaining things. […] The ruling class has figured out that a happy and productive population with free time on their hands is a mortal danger,' David Graeber (2013) writes in his essay on 'bullshit jobs'. Much of the socalled innovation that now attracts massive investment by venture capital is premised on expanding the economy of bullshit jobs. That is, bullshit in two senses—jobs that are pointless (such that they don't contribute to anything worthwhile to society) and jobs that are terrible (such that they further immiserate people). Any visions of post-capitalist futures must reckon with a technological and economic structure designed to keep much of the working class in a perpetual state of precarity and exhaustion. And in so doing, conceive of modes of production and labour that don't force human desires to compete with technological dictates, such as the robotic systems in Amazon warehouses or the algorithmic management of Uber drivers.

Conclusion

The technology sector is at the forefront of capitalist accumulation today and should be a prime focus of post-capitalist visions. Progressive politics can do much to counter the self-interested techno-utopian visions of Silicon Valley elites by conjuring radical futures based on principles of social, economic, and racial justice and attuned to questions of class. We have shown how these visions must be engaged with the current struggles and conditions of exploitation and informed by principles of resistance to the modes of capitalist exploitation. We advocate for radical futures that unsettle the balance of power and challenge the false utopianism on offer by billionaire saviours. Rather than hoping hundreds of Elon Musks and Bill Gateses will deliver a world worth living in, we all must chart an alternative path towards a world worth fighting for.

References

Fink, Larry. 2021. Letter to CEOs. *BlackRock*. https://www.blackrock.com/corporate/investor-relations/larry-fink-ceo-letter. Accessed 11 March 2021.
Fraser, Alistair. 2019. Land Grab/Data Grab: Precision Agriculture and Its New Horizons. *The Journal of Peasant Studies* 46 (5): 893–912.
Graeber, D. 2013. On the Phenomenon of Bullshit Jobs: A Work Rant. *Strike! Magazine* August 2013. https://www.strike.coop/bullshit-jobs
Illich, I. 1973. *Tools for Conviviality*. London: Harper and Row.

Lynch, Casey R. 2020. Contesting Digital Futures: Urban Politics, Alternative Economies, and the Movement for Technological Sovereignty in Barcelona. *Antipode* 52 (3): 660–680.

Morozov, Evgeny, and Francesca Bria. 2018. *Rethinking the Smart City: Democratizing Urban Technology*. New York: Rosa Luxemburg Stiftung.

Sadowski, Jathan. 2020. The Internet of Landlords: Digital Platforms and New Mechanisms of Rentier Capitalism. *Antipode* 52 (2): 562–580.

———. 2021. Future Schlock. *Real Life Magazine*. January 25. https://reallifemag.com/future-schlock/. Accessed 11 March 2021.

Yilek, C. 2021. We Need Hundreds of Elon Musks to Combat Climate Change, Bill Gates Says. *CBS News*, February 16. https://www.cbsnews.com/news/bill-gates-elon-musk-climate-change/. Accessed 10 March 2021.

11

Crises, COVID, and the Climate State

Peter Christoff

A Time of Crises

When in 1848 Marx and Engels wrote that 'all that is solid melts into air', they were referring to the liberatory effect of breaking the suffocating bonds of pre-capitalist societies' practices and beliefs. Marshall Berman has called it a description of 'the experience of modernity' (Berman 1983: 15). Many have experienced some of modernity's blessings, such as improved security, health, and welfare—products of modernity's particular forms of instrumental rationality which have been used to re-interpret, transform, and discipline our physical and social worlds.

From another perspective, however, Marx and Engels' phrase can equally be applied to the accelerating global production of greenhouse gas emissions. Many more have experienced modernity as a permanent state of crisis, or as Berman goes on to write, 'a maelstrom of perpetual disintegration and renewal, of struggle and contradiction, of ambiguity

---

P. Christoff (✉)
University of Melbourne, Parkville, VIC, Australia
e-mail: peterac@unimelb.edu.au

© The Author(s), under exclusive license to Springer Nature Singapore Pte Ltd. 2022
S. Alexander et al. (eds.), *Post-Capitalist Futures*, Alternatives and Futures: Cultures, Practices, Activism and Utopias, https://doi.org/10.1007/978-981-16-6530-1_11

and anguish' (Berman 1983: 15). This experience stretches from the devastation of Indigenous societies and cultures, to the extermination of non-human species, to the accelerating production of previously unknown threats and risks such as global economic collapse and annihilation through nuclear war. For the majority of the planet's inhabitants, human and non-human, the experience of ceaseless modernisation and capitalism's 'creative destruction' is a mounting tsunami of chaos, decreasingly glossed with hopes for a progressive future. Crises—economic, health, democratic, and ecological—now build on each other in uniquely global ways, amplifying and compounding their individual effects, and high on this list is the crisis of global warming.

The COVID-19 pandemic offers the most recent insight into this crisis-world. Importantly, for the topic of this chapter, the pandemic also has transformed, perhaps permanently, the context in which we will address the climate question. From the start of 2020, to a greater or lesser degree, depending on location and wealth, all that seemed solid melted, if not into air then, metaphorically, underfoot and then slowly congealed into new social and economic configurations that may or may not be enduring. These reconfigurations, which vary enormously by country, sometimes resemble a retreat to a slower and more geographically bounded life reminiscent of the nineteenth century or before, but they are also accompanied and enveloped by startling new arrangements that represent a reversal of many of the better achievements of globalised modernity.

As Bordoni says, 'We live in a constant state of crisis, and this crisis also involves the modern state, whose structure, functionality, effectiveness (including the system of democratic representation) are no longer suited to the times in which we live' (Bauman and Bordoni 2014: 27). This latest crisis has had profound impacts on the state—by which I mean, here, the amalgam of public apparatuses (political and legal, bureaucratic, material, and financial) that govern and shape our lives within national territorial borders. Most countries have struggled to adapt. Tough social containment measures have been implemented and legitimised using the narrative of emergency. State surveillance and regulatory controls have been strengthened to limit movement, to quarantine and to incarcerate. Previously porous borders have become almost impermeable. Expert (medical) authority has again become—as occurred during previous plagues in recent times, such as AIDS and SARS—a prominent, authoritative reference point for public policy making, although with significant variations between countries. In certain countries, however—notably the United States under Trump—pre-existing social fissures have been exacerbated and inequality amplified.

In enforcing social isolation to avert the collapse of their health systems and to reduce the death toll, some states have engineered an unnerving experience of rapid economic degrowth. In these cases, and also in states (such as the USA) where the virus has gained a powerful hold in the absence of effective defensive health measures, incomes, consumption, and production have fallen dramatically and unemployment has soared. The depth and duration of the COVID Recession remain unclear. Global economic growth fell by around 3.5 per cent in 2020, recovery is likely to be uneven, and economic projections remain uncertain (IMF 2021a). Though there remains a widespread hope that this plunge into recession is temporary and that the trajectory of the recovery of national and global capitalism will reflect the shape of the letters 'V', 'U', or 'W', it is still possible that some states—and the global economy—may still come to explore other alphabetical options, such as 'L', 'M', or 'X'.

In many states, both developed and developing (IMF 2021b), the economic shutdown has been accompanied by substantial attempts to provide a safety net to limit the social impact of the drop into the abyss, and stimulus packages to reboot economic activity. All that previously seemed impossible has suddenly become feasible as, almost overnight, core neoliberal political and economic conceptions have been set aside. The national (welfare) state has been revived and strengthened to limit health impacts, to undergird social welfare by supplementing household and corporate income, and to limit social unrest. We now have 'varieties of COVID capitalism'.

To put this in historical and geographical context, in most developed industrialised countries the past 50 years have been marked by transitions from one type of state to another. The welfare state flourished, predominantly in Europe, for 'thirty glorious years' until the mid 1970s, when increasingly insufficient tax revenue could not meet the growing demand for public infrastructure and social welfare services. The failure of this 'tax state' to fund itself led to the rise of the 'debt state': expenditure needs were met by increasing public debt, which by the late 1970s threatened to generate what were seen to be national fiscal crises. A neoliberal rebellion followed, first in English-speaking countries and then elsewhere, driven by the corporate reaction to tax demands that grew while economic growth slowed and profits declined. From the 1990s to 2008, the relative allocation of public expenditure on health, education, pensions, and welfare was reduced, public assets privatised, and tax reforms handed revenue back to the private sector. Public debt as a percentage of GDP fell throughout the OECD, as the 'consolidation state' (Wolfgang Streeck's term for the self-shrinking state) took hold. But all that reversed in 2008, following the Global Financial Crisis and its accompanying bailouts of the banking sector. In most OECD countries, the 'gains' of fiscal 'consolidation' made since the 1990s were erased. For instance, public debt in Germany and in the US, respectively, rose from 54 per cent and 9 per cent of GDP in 1995, to 69 per cent and 135 per cent in 2019 (OECD n.d.).

In all, as Streeck puts it, 'despite all attempts to conjure them away… [there are] three trends that mark the gradual decay of present-day capitalism as a socio-economic order and appear to reinforce each other in a downward spiral: *declining growth, increasing inequality,* and rising *overall debt*' (Streeck 2017: xxxiv). And, as Streeck commented in milder pre-COVID times, and summarising the main thesis of his book *Buying Time*, 'if a choice has to be made between *deflation now* and *inflation later*, or between *political unrest right away* and *bursting bubbles in the future*, there is at the end of the day no alternative left but to try to buy more time, in the hope for a miracle of some kind happening along the way' (Streeck 2017: xli, emphasis in original).

Desperate times have again called for desperate measures. This renewed trajectory towards growing debt has been dramatically enhanced by the COVID crisis, following interventions by the US Federal Reserve, the European Central Bank, the Bank of England and others. The political sphere appears to have reasserted its dominance over the economy as states have been summoned to provide welfare assistance and bail out small businesses to avert economic collapse and social chaos. In a radical turn to hyper-Keynesian intervention, the remaining ideological barriers to elevated public debt have fallen away, at least for now. The OECD reports that:

> [among OECD countries, during 2020 alone] central government debt is expected to increase from USD 47 trillion to USD 52.7 trillion at the end of 2020. At the same time, OECD economies, facing the deepest recession since the 1930s, are projected to contract by 7.5% in 2020, under a single hit scenario which assumes a successful resolution of the current outbreak. ... Central government marketable debt-to-GDP ratio for the OECD is projected to rise by 13.4 percentage points to around 86% in 2020. For comparison purposes, this ratio rose by 12.6 percentage points between 2007 and 2009, during the global financial crisis. (OECD 2020: 5)

Importantly, this most recent attempt to 'buy time' may have profound implications for individual countries' future ability to respond to the threat of climate change. Much depends on whether or not there is a global shift in attitude among policy makers, political elites, and the public, towards accepting the legitimacy of these new levels of public debt, and agreement that such a high level of public debt is sustainable and indeed may be further extended. If the supporters of Modern Monetary Theory gain in influence then this significant increase in crisis-related debt will be regarded merely as an opportunity for further debt-funded 'productive' public expenditure. However, if this view does *not* take hold, then this massive increase in public debt—alongside already elevated levels of public and private debt—will be seen to limit the fiscal capacity of states to further intervene and will encourage austerity measures such as the absolute reduction of public services and welfare as well as increases in taxation. Green New Deals have the potential to thrive or to fail to materialise, accordingly.

The Climate State

Just as the 2008 Global Financial Crisis fatally undermined progress towards the 2009 UN Copenhagen Agreement, setting back negotiations by six crucial years, so too the COVID pandemic has forced the deferral of the United Nations Framework Convention on Climate Change (UNFCCC)'s 2020 Glasgow COP until 2021 and distracted political attention from the demands of the Paris Agreement at a crucial time for negotiating new, tougher emissions targets for 2030 and beyond.

Over the past decade, climate scientists and then politicians have come to agree that global average warming of 1.5 °C, and certainly warming above 2 °C, may bring catastrophic social, economic, and ecological changes. To have better than a 50 per cent chance of keeping warming below 1.5 °C—the absurdly high-risk assumption embedded in the Paris Agreement—global emissions must be lowered to net zero shortly after the middle of this century. The goal of Net Zero by 2050 or thereabouts is far less important than the volume of emissions produced in getting there. The effective emissions pathway to such an outcome involves 'halving gross anthropogenic carbon dioxide emissions every decade' (Rockström et al. 2017). This trajectory is going to be difficult to achieve. Even with the crash in global emissions predicted to result from the COVID Recession, persistent high emissions levels have reduced the global carbon budget (UNEP 2019) to the point where the transition to renewables must occur before 2050 if warming is to be restrained.

Unfortunately, the rate and amount of private sector investment in renewable energy systems—although accelerating since the turn of this century—remains insufficient to meet this schedule for emissions reduction. The International Renewable Energy Agency (IRENA) and Climate Policy Initiative (CPI) recently indicated that '[global] annual investment in renewables would need to almost triple from an average of just below US$300 billion in 2013–2018 to almost US$800 billion by 2050' to fulfil key global decarbonisation and climate goals (IRENA/CPI 2020: 12).

For a timely transition, therefore, states will most likely have to invest directly in decarbonisation and also help cover the costs of related stranded assets. These public costs are likely to be high, especially if they follow a just transition strategy essential to maintain political support: total investment required to hold global warming to below 2 °C has been conservatively estimated to be around US$95 trillion between 2016 and 2030 (OECD 2017). The costs are growing as the time available for holding global warming below 2 °C continues to shrink. It is here that the spectre of state debt becomes relevant. If major emitting states are unprepared to spend, guide, and drive investment into ending fossil fuel use within a decade or so—because technical or political impediments to raising further revenue or generating further debt prevail—even higher levels of global warming will be locked in. Failing to make the transition in time, and with extreme weather events on the rise, the costs to the state will become greater still.

The term *welfare state* describes the dominant 'purpose' of a type of state, namely, to provide welfare to its citizens. In recent times, concepts like *environmental welfare state* and the *green state* have extended this idea to describe states offering recognition to and governance of human impacts on the non-human world (Christoff 2005; Eckersley 2004). The idea of the *climate state* shifts the focus from the welfare state's anthropocentric goals to the state's socio-ecological challenges. Just as welfare is the predominant 'purpose' of one state type, the *climate state* is governed by a specific and critical task: responding to climate change is its defining characteristic because it will become our collective overriding preoccupation, *for better or worse*.

Why burden the state with yet another label? Clearly, many states are reluctant, poorly prepared, and have limited capacities for dealing with the climate challenge. On the one hand, it is necessary to highlight global heating's challenge to state capacity and its overwhelming power to (re) frame the future of the state and indeed the international state system. On the other, this reframing illuminates the ways in which the structure, functionality, and effectiveness of states of all sorts are being transformed by climate change—not necessarily for the better.

The climate state has been emerging over the past two decades, in response to the challenge of mitigating emissions, and adapting to climate impacts and repairing the damage. Evidence for this may be found in the state's strategic and material role in the decarbonisation of national energy systems, and in guiding responses to longer-term changes such as sea level rise, and changes to temperatures and rainfall and therefore food availability. It is found in the evolving fabric of climate law, and legally mandated national emissions targets and adaptation plans. Critically, states increasingly confront the social impacts and economic and ecological losses of extreme events, such as fires, floods, and storms intensified by global heating. Here the state is being called to be—where possible—the insurer and provider of last resort, rebuilding and repairing public infrastructure but also providing increasing financial assistance to the private sector in times of disaster, and assistance in restraining the ecological catastrophe that warming will deliver. Last, the state is being increasingly called upon to deal with population movements—internal and transboundary—propelled by global heating. These roles—specifically those relating to adaptation, loss, and damage, and managing the security consequences of a warming world—will endure well beyond the mitigation challenge, and security rather than welfare will be the predominant concern.

Climate Capitalist Futures?

At this point in time, the world of climate states may still evolve in one of two broad directions. Intense activity over the next decade by the 20 major emitting states and effective international cooperation now may head off the worst impacts of global warming. Domestic emissions will need to be quickly reduced to zero alongside a rapid end to the extraction, use, and trade in coal, gas, and oil. This dramatic shift will still leave states to deal—as a matter of priority—with the consequences of already established warming. Such adaptation may occur through equitable burden sharing, or through a further intensification of inequality, within and beyond state borders.

Even so, there will be individual states that may succumb to the compounding impacts of scarcity caused by water and food shortages, extreme events, sea level rise, and population movements. In this better alternative future, capitalism may survive, generally in a form strictly disciplined and driven by climatic constraints, but potentially still as destructive across a wide range of other ecological and social values as it is at present.

However, if the attempts to hold warming to below 2 °C fail, then it is more likely that states will come to exist in a turbulent and rising sea of domestic unrest and international conflict. In this alternative future, surviving states may remain domestically socially cohesive—think of the Scandinavian welfare states—or may become deeply oppressive and increasingly authoritarian. But they will be outwardly fiercely militarised and, insofar as they deliver welfare and protection to their human and non-human inhabitants, in many ways they will most likely be shadows of their former identities. At best, this second path involves a return to a form of mercantilism, with realms of the planet profoundly immiserated and reduced to warlordism. By this stage, what remains of the global capitalist system that drove them to this outcome will be the least of our concerns.

References

Bauman, Zygmunt, and Carlo Bordoni. 2014. *State of Crisis*. Cambridge: Polity.

Berman, Marshall. 1983. *All that is Solid Melts into Air*. London: Verso.

Christoff, Peter. 2005. Out of Chaos, a Shining Star? Toward a Typology of Green States. In *The State and the Global Ecological Crisis*, ed. John Barry and Robyn Eckersley. Cambridge, MA: MIT Press.

Eckersley, Robyn. 2004. *The Green State: Rethinking Democracy and Sovereignty*. Cambridge, MA: MIT Press.

IMF (International Monetary Fund). 2021a. *World Economic Outlook Update: January 2021*. https://www.imf.org/en/Publications/WEO/Issues/2021/01/26/2021-world-economic-outlook-update. Accessed 18 Dec 2020.

———. 2021b. *Policy Responses to COVID*. https://www.imf.org/en/Topics/imf-and-covid19/Policy-Responses-to-COVID-19. Accessed 18 Dec 2020.

IRENA (International Renewable Energy Agency)/ CPI (Climate Policy Initiative). 2020. *Global Landscape of Renewable Energy Finance 2020*.

OECD. 2017. *Investing in Climate, Investing in Growth*. https://www.oecd.org/environment/cc/g20-climate/synthesis-investing-in-climate-investing-in-growth.pdf. Accessed 18 Dec 2020.

———. 2020. *Sovereign Borrowing Outlook for OECD Countries 2020: Special COVID-19 Edition*. Paris: OECD.

———. n.d. *General Government Debt*. https://data.oecd.org/gga/general-government-debt.htm. Accessed 18 Dec 2020.

Rockström, Johan, Owen Gaffney, Joeri Rogelj, Malte Meinshausen, Nebojsa Nakicenovic, and Hans Joachim Schellnhuber. 2017. A Roadmap for Rapid Decarbonization. *Science* 24: 1269.

Streeck, Wolfgang. 2017. *Buying Time: The Delayed Crisis of Democratic Capitalism*. 2nd ed. London: Verso.
UNEP. 2019. *Emissions Gap Report 2019*. https://www.unenvironment.org/resources/emissions-gap-report-2019. Accessed 18 Dec 2020.

Part III

Post-Capitalist Geographies and Resistance

12

Localisation: The World Beyond Capitalism

Helena Norberg-Hodge

I'm pleased that the editors of this volume chose to describe what lies beyond capitalism using the plural—'futures'—rather than implying that a single alternative will be appropriate for all people in all places. I've had the unusual opportunity of studying the impact of the globalising economy on diverse cultures—from the least industrialised to the most industrialised—over the past 40 years. In about a dozen countries, from Sweden, Spain, and the USA, to Bhutan, India, and South Korea, I've had ongoing working relationships over most of this period. In addition, as a co-founder of the International Forum on Globalisation, I was able to meet with about 40 colleagues from every continent, who were studying the impact of free trade treaties, or globalisation, on their countries.

From these experiences it became absolutely clear that one of our most urgent tasks is to recognise the fundamental importance of diversity, both cultural and biological. Respecting and strengthening diversity means

---

H. Norberg-Hodge (✉)
Local Futures and The International Alliance for Localisation,
East Hardwick, VT, USA
e-mail: hnh@localfutures.org

dismantling the economic structures that have imposed a monoculture worldwide and rebuilding those structures in ways that allow economic activity to adapt to local cultures, climates, soils, and resources. This adaptation to diversity offers the hope of a *plurality* of futures that meet genuine human needs without destroying our only living planet.

Post-capitalist futures are what can emerge when the invisible hand of the global economy releases its grip on communities and ecosystems around the world, allowing local networks of mutual interdependence to thrive. Reducing the economic and psychological pressures that tie us into dependence on distant corporate entities will help liberate humanity's innovative genius to respond to the complex challenges of particular ecosystems and communities, rather than forcing people to compete for the same artificially scarce livelihoods and resources. There is absolutely no shortage of work on this planet. People have been made dependent on centralised institutions that control the allocation of jobs, money, and manufactured goods.

During the 2020 coronavirus pandemic, many centralised institutions failed to protect the most vulnerable. Instead, self-organised community groups emerged all over the world to coordinate grocery and medicine deliveries, to look after the aged and the infirm, and to help provide for those who lost their jobs. These mutual aid groups demonstrated the caring, compassionate side of human nature (Sitrin and Sembra 2020). That same side was also revealed when previously atomised residents of many locked-down neighbourhoods began singing and making music for one another from balconies, open windows, and across streets.

In this period there was also a huge awakening to the fundamental importance of being more self-reliant in food. In countless communities, the sale of seedlings and garden tools skyrocketed as people planted vegetable gardens. And while supermarket shelves were often left empty for days on end, smaller farms linked to the local market prospered, and restaurants were transformed into 'food hubs' for the preparation and distribution of locally produced food.[1]

These trends may have been accelerated by the pandemic, but they have been underway for more than a decade. We are, in fact, witnessing

---

[1] Many more examples are here: https://www.localfutures.org/covid-19/.

the co-creation of post-capitalist futures all around the world. This is a movement comprised of people who have begun to see through the increasingly shallow façade of consumer capitalism, and now recognise that *connection*, both to others and to Nature, is the true wellspring of happiness. They are withdrawing their dependence on the global economy and, from the ground up, re-inventing more direct social and cultural arrangements by renewing local economies.

A proliferation of such renewal initiatives—farmers' markets, community gardens and co-ops, local business alliances, community investment schemes, alternative learning projects, and countless others—are demonstrating the profound ecological, economic, social, and health benefits of reweaving relationships at the local level.[2] Local food initiatives, in particular, are proving that we can stimulate widespread agricultural diversification and job-rich ecological farming simply by shortening the distances between producer and consumer. These efforts are simultaneously boosting agricultural productivity, restoring ecosystems, providing habitat for wildlife, and generating meaningful employment.

Renewal initiatives are also demonstrating the incredible healing power of deep, intergenerational community. Studies are revealing that the epidemics of depression, anxiety, and addiction afflicting people worldwide are linked to the social atomisation endemic to modern, globalised society (Walker 2007; Hari 2018). At the same time, the therapies that successfully treat such afflictions—such as 12-step programmes, therapeutic horticulture, and an array of wilderness-immersion therapies—invariably involve the strengthening of social relationships and/or reconnection to the natural world. In the course of observing many such projects, I have seen prisoners and delinquent teenagers transformed and social, ethnic, and intergenerational rifts bridged.

Given these and other benefits, I'm convinced that genuinely healthy, happy, and ecologically regenerative futures must not only be post-capitalist; they must also be post-*centralist*, post-*globalist*, post-*urbanist*, and post-*industrialist*—in other words, more *localised*. To succeed, post-capitalist economies need to bring the economy back home—back to

---

[2] For a snapshot of the diversity and breadth of these initiatives, see: https://www.localfutures.org/programs/global-to-local/planet-local/.

within people's clear view, back to a level small enough in scale and scope that exploitation of others and of the environment can be easily apprehended by the community, enabling people to take responsibility for their own actions.

Of course, getting the global economy to release its immobilising grip is the biggest challenge in the unfolding of healthy futures. It is therefore necessary to engage not only in renewal, but also in resistance, at a level sufficient to the task of breaking up corporate power. This will require forging an ever-broadening coalition of people's movements, with the aim of halting current destruction and protecting the local, globally. Because nation-states are the smallest unit of governance capable of reining in global corporations and banks, we will need to reclaim and marshal the power of the state to enforce a range of rules, regulations, bans, and other policies that can constrain globalised capital. At the same time, the economic supports—primarily taxes, subsidies, and regulations—that are currently afforded to monopolies in the global economy need to be redirected towards local economies.

I want to point out here that it is possible to demand that the nation state regulate corporations while simultaneously devolving power to the regions. This will be much clearer to people once they are informed about the fact that governments at the moment are simultaneously deregulating global corporations while over-regulating local and national enterprises.

These strategies of *resistance* are necessary both to halt current destruction and to enable *renewal* initiatives to flourish. In the remainder of this chapter, I will focus on some of the key areas requiring fundamental, structural change.

Land and Farming

The war against independent local economies reached its peak in the eighteenth and nineteenth centuries with the dispossession of people from the land, via the Enclosures in Europe, and through European conquest and colonialism in much of the rest of the world. In both cases, previously self-reliant people were forced off their land and either into cities where they worked as wage labourers for an industrialising economy, or as slaves on monocultural export-oriented plantations.

This process of dispossession continues today: from land-grabbing to forced labour, from real estate speculation to suburban sprawl development. The struggle for survivable futures will therefore need to resist and reverse the destruction of rural self-reliance. This is necessary to avoid an acceleration of ecological destruction and an increase in social unrest. This is the struggle at the heart of the global food sovereignty movement, currently spearheaded by the world's largest social movement, La Via Campesina.[3]

Protecting or rebuilding economies of sufficiency leads inevitably to the issue of urbanisation, a process currently advancing at a runaway pace thanks to policies promoting economic globalisation. Mass urbanisation has many costs. It transforms hundreds of millions of previously land-based people into urban consumers, thereby accelerating the depletion of resources and adding to pollution of all sorts, including greenhouse gases. By cutting off members of diverse ethnic and religious groups from their own communities and into cutthroat competition with others for survival, it is also exacerbating conflict and strife.

'Smart cities' are being promoted as the path to a sustainable future. But a broader, more global view reveals that pulling the nearly half of humanity that still lives in close connection to the land into exploding cities may offer healthy returns for global capital, but for people and the planet it is sheer madness. It is vital that we raise awareness about this central issue and build North/South movements to resist the process.

A vision of a more agrarian future can be off-putting for many people, who have been trained to believe that farm work means drudgery, and that 'progress' means a transcendence of manual labour. In fact, it is essential that we question the central narrative of progress, which assumes that industrialisation has liberated humanity from toil in the fields. This assumption comes out of a myopic understanding of agriculture. For serfs and for slaves, work on the land was, no doubt, hard and brutish.

---

[3] La Via Campesina is a movement of 182 local and national organisations in 81 countries, representing some 200 million peasants, small-scale farmers, agricultural workers, and indigenous peoples, promoting food sovereignty and agroecology, and resisting agribusiness. See: https://viacampesina.org/en/international-peasants-voice/, and Desmarais (2006).

Similarly, the post-colonial, globalised food economy means monocultures grown for export and managed by a single farmer operating huge machinery, often with the help of migrant labour. The work is invariably monotonous, disempowering, and culturally marginalised.

However, in many parts of the world there have been examples of traditional, family farms that provided satisfying livelihoods for generations. In the past few decades, the emerging worldwide local food movement is being created by individuals who have developed a deep appreciation of land-based work. Local food systems provide fuller employment, more varied, meaningful work, fairly treated farm workers, revitalised rural communities, ecological restoration, and more beautiful futures. An Australian farmer once encapsulated this poignantly to me; 'I've been a farmer all my life, and I've felt like a serf,' he explained. This all changed radically when he began selling at a local farmer's market, rather than via the global agribusiness-dominated market. He went from growing just two commodities—for which the price was dictated by monopolistic supermarket procurers as a tiny fraction of the sale price—to more than 20 different products, for which 100% of the sale price goes to him and his employees. He experiences weekly, face-to-face contact with his consumers. 'It's like entering a new galaxy,' he told me, beaming as he spoke.

It is no wonder, then, that we are now witnessing a surge of interest in community-based, diversified farming and local markets—despite the fact that these receive almost no support from governments and almost no attention from mainstream media and academia. From Australia and the UK to India, Palestine, and the US, young farmers' movements are growing; in big cities and rural towns alike, farmers' markets, consumer-producer cooperatives, and community gardens are reconnecting people with the sources of their food, strengthening local economies, and reducing environmental impact. In contrast to the widespread stereotype of farming towns as narrow-minded backwaters, these localising communities are hubs of cultural vitality and open-heartedness.

Post-Global Business

Thanks to 'free trade' treaties, corporations are currently able to scour the planet seeking the cheapest labour, the lowest taxes, and the least stringent environmental rules—which drives wages and environmental protection down to the lowest common denominator. In more localised post-capitalist economies, businesses will instead be place based; they will abide by the rules established by society rather than societies worldwide bending to the wishes of global business.

Regulating transnational corporations requires new trade treaties in which governments agree to re-regulate instead of de-regulating global trade and finance. Of particular importance is to immediately ban the odious 'investor-state dispute settlement' (ISDS) rules that allow corporations to sue governments over laws or regulations that might impede corporate profiteering.[4] We need to support protectionism: governments and communities must be allowed to protect their communities and environments from exploitation.

None of this means that regional and international trade would entirely disappear, but such trade would primarily involve exchanges of surpluses once local needs are met, for goods that cannot be produced locally. Nor does it mean that there would be no large-scale industrial production. A certain efficiency of scale applies to the manufacture of mechanical and technological products like trains and computers, and these will still require centralised production (though at lower levels than at present).

But it's important to emphasise that similar 'efficiencies of scale' do not apply to farming, fishing, and forestry, which are actually *more* efficient at smaller scale (Jensen 2016). The so-called efficiency of large-scale production is measured in terms of production per unit of labour, not per unit of land, energy, and resources. In other words, production practices that increase unemployment, pollution, and resource depletion are perversely described as more 'efficient'.

In a transition to post-capitalist futures, small businesses and local business alliances play a key role in bolstering community self-reliance.

---

[4] See resources at the Corporate Europe Observatory here: https://corporateeurope.org/en/international-trade/2019/01/investor-privileges-vs-people-and-planet.

And there are many alternative business structures to replace the corporation, including cooperatives, not-for-profit businesses, social enterprises, etc., all forming part of a 'degrowth business' framework and practice (Nesterova 2020). These alternatives all contain elements of a post-capitalist vision: democratic ownership, control and decision-making, and subordination of profit to social and ecological values. Communities should determine the kind of business structures that make sense for them, but these should operate on a small-enough scale to ensure transparency and accountability.

Finance and Money

As things stand today, private banks are empowered to create money through the issuance of debt. These loans must be repaid with interest, helping drive the global economy's need for endless growth, and the accelerating extraction and exploitation needed to ensure it.

Fortunately, people around the world are resisting that system through boycott and divestment movements, legal advocacy, 'move your money' and debt jubilee campaigns, and more. They are also exploring and practising alternatives that subordinate money accumulation to the genuine needs of people, communities, and nature, including public banks, local investment funds, slow money, regenerative finance, and others.

There is also ongoing experimentation with local currencies, time banks, and other complementary currency schemes. After having worked closely with such initiatives and witnessed their evolution, I have concluded that they are most effective when the economy of our basic needs has already been significantly localised (Norberg-Hodge 2000).

Post-Consumerism

To meet the needs of expansionist industry, modern capitalism depends in large measure upon manufacturing discontentment, for which a marketed product is presented as the 'solution'. This endless process—the central feature of consumerism—undermines the wellbeing of the very individuals the system is purported to serve, even as it engulfs the living planet in a conflagration of destruction. The most tragic failing of our global economic system is that it is eviscerating the Earth itself for the systematic production of unhappiness.

Creating post-capitalist economies will require dismantling the consumer culture and its primary drivers, the hundreds of billions of dollars per year advertising and marketing industry. This will require numerous political actions in concert with the broader regulation of corporations described above, starting with the banning of adverts targeting children.

In post-capitalist futures, cultures will want goods of maximum durability. This means an end to that key support for consumerism—planned obsolescence. Repair will not only be decriminalised (it's actually illegal to repair some devices and machines today) and encouraged, but product designs will be required to maximise repairability, reusability, refurbishability—and importantly, biodegradability.

These shifts would lead to a flourishing of artisanal crafts and careful use of natural, place-based materials. In place of consumerism, individuals would increase their creativity and develop multiple skills. In such community-based economies, people would lead rich and diverse lives, shored up by webs of relationship and interdependence that provide for the fundamental need of belonging, meaning, and satisfaction.

Reducing Energy Consumption and Reigning in Tech

Post-consumerist cultures and post-capitalist economies clearly need to reduce energy consumption. One obvious place to start would be to halt the current practice of 'redundant trade', in which countries routinely import *and export* near-identical quantities of products, wasting an enormous amount of energy and adding needlessly to pollution (Keller 2019).

Energy would come from decentralised renewable energy sources, including solar, hydro, biogas, and wind. While there is increasing debate about the actual ecological and social impacts of large-scale renewable energy plants, a myriad of existing local energy projects around the world are proving that smaller-scale solutions do not disrupt local ecosystems, and have the added benefit of bolstering community fabric.

Of course, the immense technological development required by global capitalism cannot be powered by small-scale plants. In my opinion, that's a very good thing. Technological development under capitalism is both socially corrosive (of freedom, democracy, justice, community, and human wellbeing), and ecologically devastating (consider the mines, toxic pollution, e-waste, energy-and-water-guzzling data centres, etc., behind today's digital technologies) (Suarez-Villa 2009).

If we hope to make sane and healthy futures possible, I believe that we ultimately need to arrest further expansion and speed of communications technologies, including the internet and digital technology, and scale back their use in business. This is not an 'anti-technology' stance that attempts to end all technological development. But what's needed are genuinely *decentralised* tools, not still more centralised technologies that amplify the power of monopolistic businesses while magnifying our impact on the natural world. Shifting the focus of technological development away from profit-maximisation offers the prospect of putting humanity's creativity to the task of maximising quality of life while simultaneously minimising ecological harm.

Localising, Globally

To be clear, the localisation necessary for just and healthy futures must be firmly internationalist and distinguish itself from right-wing nationalism or xenophobia. In fact, globalisation has exacerbated those troubling trends. All over the world, from Australia to Bhutan, from Wales to Ladakh, I have seen how competition for scarce jobs and resources in the global economy, coupled with a consumer culture that imbues people with a deep sense of inadequacy, has precipitated dramatic increases in intolerance, xenophobia, fundamentalism, and factional conflict. By creating more secure livelihoods and more vital cultures, localisation is key in transcending divisiveness and competition, and contributing to contentment, openness, and tolerance.

What's more, international cooperation and cross-border information exchange between grassroots groups are necessary for the building up of a people's movement powerful enough to reverse corporate globalisation and to bring about localised post-capitalist futures. This international exchange is already happening.[5] The localisation movement and other closely affiliated movements—new economies, food sovereignty, regenerative agriculture, simplicity, commons, degrowth, and so on—are forming international alliances. Importantly, they are linking hands with the land-based and indigenous peoples of the world who have been able to resist the pressures of globalisation and continue to practice self provisioning, reciprocal care, mutual exchange, and 'buen vivir'. These ancient cultures are vital sources of knowledge, telling us that it is possible to meet human needs within the limits of nature.

They also reveal the central importance of transcending capitalism's desacralised worldview (Heilbroner 1985). While global capital has made people almost everywhere dependent on unaccountable corporations and anonymous producers on the other side of the world, localisation creates mutual interdependence within community and a particular place. In this way, localisation puts us back in contact with the constantly evolving, changing nature of the universe—we become aware that every person, animal, and plant is unique and changing from moment to moment. Localisation lends us the intimacy and pace required to feel this fullness, and to feel the joy of being an integral part of a living web of relationships

Acknowledgements I'd like to thank Alex Jensen for considerable assistance when drafting this chapter.

---

[5] See: https://www.localfutures.org/programs/global-to-local/international-alliance-localization/.

References

Desmarais, Annette Aurélie. 2006. *La Via Campesina: Globalization and the Power of Peasants*. Nova Scotia: Fernwood Publishing.

Hari, Johann. 2018. *Lost Connections: Uncovering the Real Causes of Depression—and the Unexpected Solutions*. New York: Bloomsbury.

Heilbroner, Robert. 1985. *The Nature and Logic of Capitalism*. New York: W.W. Norton & Company.

Jensen, Alex. 2016. Energy Efficiency in Agriculture: Agro-Ecological Vs Industrial Farms. *Farmers' Forum* 16 (6): 30–35.

Keller, Sean. 2019. Connecting the Dots: Insane Trade and Climate Chaos. *Local Futures blog*. Accessed December 18, 2020. https://www.localfutures.org/connecting-the-dots-insane-trade-and-climate-chaos/.

Nesterova, Iana. 2020. Degrowth Business Framework: Implications for Sustainable Development. *Journal of Cleaner Production* 262. https://doi.org/10.1016/j.clepro.2020.121382.

Norberg-Hodge, Helena. 2000. *Ancient Futures: Learning from Ladakh*. London: Rider Books.

Sitrin, Marina, and Collectiva Sembra. 2020. *Pandemic Solidarity: Mutual Aid during the Covid-19 Crisis*. London: Pluto Press.

Suarez-Villa, Luis. 2009. *Technocapitalism: A Critical Perspective on Technological Innovation and Corporatism*. Philadelphia: Temple University Press.

Walker, Carl. 2007. *Depression and Globalization: The Politics of Mental Health in the 21st Century*. New York: Springer-Verlag.

13

Indigenous Australians and Their Lands: Post-Capitalist Development Alternatives

Jon Altman

> *But I must add that, apart from the splendid mineral, pastoral, and agricultural possibilities in the Territory, which will enable it to become populous, progressive, and productive, we must remember that in its proper development lies the key, not only to the defence of Australia, but to the development of its north. About one-half of Australia lies north of a line running from the Gascoyne River to Gladstone. Is this half to be neglected? … Either we must accomplish the peopling of the Northern Territory or submit to its transfer to some other nation. The latter alternative is not to be tolerated. The Territory must be peopled by a white race.*
> —Alfred Deakin in debate over the Northern Territory Acceptance Bill, Australian parliament, Hansard 15 October 1909

In this chapter I want to focus on post-capitalist development alternatives for Indigenous peoples on their legally repossessed lands that currently cover more than half of continental Australia. Axiomatic to my analysis is

---

J. Altman (✉)
School of Regulation and Global Governance, The Australian National University, Canberra, ACT, Australia
e-mail: Jon.Altman@anu.edu.au

the notion of economic hybridity or plurality that highlights the resilience and continuity of customary non-capitalist relations of production in remote Indigenous Australia.

The epigram at the beginning is by a very powerful white Australian, Alfred Deakin, who was thrice prime minister of the nation in the early twentieth century. One hundred and ten years later, thinking about the capitalist development of Aboriginal lands, mainly in what is termed in the discourse of the dominant, 'remote' Australia has changed little. Settler colonialism from 1788 saw Indigenous peoples violently and illegally dispossessed of their land. As historian Patrick Wolfe (2006) astutely observed, the logic of the Australian settler colonial formation was premised on displacing Indigenous people from the land and this was a project completed very effectively. In some geographically remote locations, land deemed of no commercial value was reserved for exclusive Aboriginal use; in such situations Indigenous people were corralled in government settlements and missions for administrative ease and to curtail their pre-colonial mobility so as to prepare them for imagined assimilation into the capitalist economy and society.

From 1788, there was the replacement of one economic system—based on hunting, fishing, gathering, and arguably some incipient agriculture, supporting at best guess around 750,000 people continentally—with capitalism, which today supports a national population of 25 million people at a far higher material standard of living. But the sustainability of the current system is broken, nationally and globally, as a combination of climate change, global warming, pandemic disruption to globalisation, resource depletion, and escalating inequality all coalesce. And Australia is doing its bit to assist the demise of capitalism as we know it: the nation's wealth has been built on extraction of natural capital via industrial agriculture with disastrous environmental impacts, and extraction of non-renewable mineral wealth, including coal, oil, and gas, that both domestically and globally are contributing to carbon pollution and the overheating of the planet.

From an Indigenous perspective we have seen three historic trends.

The first was the rapid decline and then recovery of the Indigenous population as currently defined (focusing on self-identification, ancestry, and community acceptance). The Indigenous population today of

800,000 (as estimated in the 2016 Census) probably exceeds that of 1788, which had declined to just over 100,000 at the beginning of the twentieth century. But today's population is differently distributed, being mainly urbanised, and differently ethnically constituted, with many Indigenous people being of diverse ethnicity and layered identity.

The second trend that is very apparent in the past 50 years is the socio-economic disparities between Indigenous and other Australians; these disparities are documented in every five-yearly census since 1971, when Indigenous people were first made statistically visible. Despite concerted government efforts to reduce these disparities, a policy framework referred to officially since 2008 as 'Closing the Gap', 'gaps' have not closed, with some, like formal employment and individual incomes, proving intractable. It is noteworthy that these disparities are greatest in remote Australia where only three in 10 adults have employment and where, paradoxically, Indigenous people have repossessed the most land. This situation is comprehensively documented in regular reports by Australia's Productivity Commission and in annual reports to the Australian parliament.

The third trend central to this chapter's focus is the rapid growth in land repossession, what is arguably a 'land titling revolution' evident since the late 1960s (Altman and Markham 2015). Under statutory land rights laws passed in the Northern Territory and South Australia in the 1970s and 1980s, nearly 800,000 sq. kms of land (10 per cent of Australia) has been granted as Aboriginal inalienable freehold title. In these two jurisdictions, landowners enjoyed forms of free prior and informed consent rights that have provided considerable control over commercial developments on their lands. After the *Mabo* High Court judgment in 1992 and the passage of the Commonwealth's Native Title Act in 1993, considerable tracts of land have been successfully determined: as of April 2020 one million sq. kms (14 per cent of Australia) is under exclusive native title possession and two million sq. kms (29 per cent of Australia) is under non-exclusive native title that is shared with other land occupiers. All told, over half the continent is currently under some form of Indigenous title, but the property rights attenuated to such title is highly variable ranging from being relatively strong with land rights and informed consent rights to relatively weak with native title where mineral extraction rights take precedence over native title rights and interests that at best are financially compensable when extinguished.

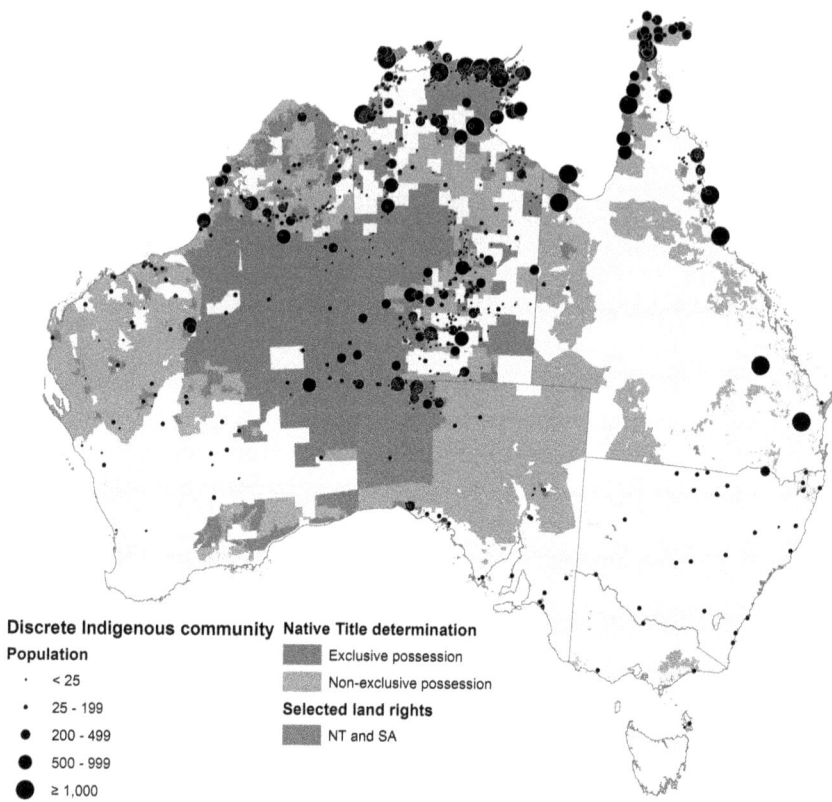

Fig. 13.1 Aboriginal titled lands and discrete Indigenous communities in 2020. (Data sources: Altman and Markham (2015) updated by Dr Francis Markham with information from the 2016 Census and the National Native Title Tribunal http://www.nntt.gov.au/Maps/Determinations_map.pdf, accessed 3 June 2020)

In Fig. 13.1 the spatial coverage of Indigenous titled lands and the location of 1,200 discrete Indigenous communities (so defined by the Australian Bureau of Statistics because of their majority Indigenous population) are illustrated. The correlation between recovered lands and a growing Indigenous population are poorly correlated—the population of these communities comprises 20 per cent of the total Indigenous population at most. Most Indigenous people do not live on Indigenous-titled lands. And those who do must first bear an onus to legally prove a continuity of connection with the land since colonisation and a continuity of land-holding customs and traditions: if they are to successfully claim back their lands they need to legally demonstrate what is tantamount to a fiction of 'uninvadedness' (Wolfe 2006). In places where people have exclusive land rights and native title possession, where they are most 'uninvaded', they constitute over 80 per cent of the population.

My focus here is on post-capitalist possibilities on these repossessed lands, possibilities limited by the absence of property rights in sub-surface minerals that are deemed too modern to be recognised in the terms that native title allows. Nor are Indigenous lands granted distinct political jurisdiction, with landowners and residents subject to the settler sovereign state assertion that as citizens they must comply with western, not customary, law—despite needing to deploy custom to prove rightful land ownership.

The settler state's aspiration to develop remote Australia, as articulated by Deakin in 1909 and repeated throughout the twentieth century, has been rekindled in the twenty-first century with powerful discourse in a parliamentary White Paper about 'developing the north' (Australian Government 2015). But it is rarely mentioned in such manifestos that most of the north, outside urban centres and mining towns, is Aboriginal-titled and peopled. Such policy focus imagines a capitalist future that sees mineral and agricultural extraction that has occurred in the more densely settled and temperate parts of Australia, with considerable environmental damage, seamlessly replicated in inhospitable desert and tropical Australia. This dominant political view wrongly assumes that geography and climate do not matter. It also assumes that culture is irrelevant, so ignoring the reality that those who hold native title generally abide by different norms and values than other Australians and that their rights and interests, minerals aside, are legally recognised. The law states that such rights are compensable, if extinguished, or protected, if limited to domestic use. There is a dominant view that the market and non-market can somehow be neatly bifurcated, which is erroneous especially with indistinguishable natural resources like fresh water and fisheries.

There is clear historical evidence that in the political-economic struggle over mineral resources the interests of corporate entities and the settler state take precedence over Indigenous human flourishing. From an

Indigenous standpoint, mining is inevitably destructive of the sacred geography recently recognised and reclaimed—extractive mining destroys what is a sentient, living landscape for Indigenous landowners. And while there is some evidence of employment and enterprise benefits from mining for Indigenous people, the 2016 Census shows just 6,650 Indigenous mine workers nationally. And mine work is highly vulnerable to automation. Nevertheless, much Indigenous-titled land remains largely unexplored and assumed highly prospective; there is a danger that recent Indigenous re-possession will be followed by re-dispossession.

History also shows that forms of state and missionary capitalism failed in remote Australia, and what has succeeded has been dependent on heavy state subsidisation over many years as currently evidenced in the multi-billion dollars Northern Australia Infrastructure Facility. Still, the aspirations of corporate and political elites for grand schemes of industrial agriculture, aquaculture, and mineral extraction persist. This is despite climatic projections published regularly by the Australia Institute, a Canberra-based think tank, that show that the number of days over 35 °C are likely to increase rapidly. For example, in Darwin, the capital of the Northern Territory, the number of such days has increased from a recorded 5–6 in the early twentieth century to 20 in the early twenty-first century to a forecasted 132 by 2030 and 275 by 2070: the 'white race' that Deakin referred to in 1909 will not find such conditions conducive to habitation or labouring.

There are other options already embraced by Indigenous landowners that are indicative of post-capitalist possibilities. Intensive commercial agriculture has been largely absent from remote Australia for many reasons, including an inhospitable environment and lack of water, especially in the desert, and remoteness, itself defined in relation to metropolitan centres of commerce. The main form of agricultural extraction in remote Australia is and was cattle ranching over massive, leased stations, some the size of European countries, many historically exploiting Indigenous labour. Much of the north of low commercial value was unalienated and remained under crown ownership. It was for this reason that it became available for claim under land rights and native title laws. And because it was not intensively exploited, this part of Australia retains high environmental values.

Over the last two decades Indigenous landowners have voluntarily committed massive tracts of their land with high conservation and biodiversity values into the National Reserve System. These high values accord with International Union for the Conservation of Nature criteria and help Australia meet key international commitments made under the United Nations Convention on Biological Diversity since 1992. There are currently 75 Indigenous Protected Areas declared, with 12 more in the consultation phase. Indigenous lands committed to conservation total about 1 million sq. kms and constitute over half of Australia's conservation estate, operating as a massive, at times contiguous, conservation commons.

While these conservation lands are relatively environmentally intact, they face many destructive threats from invasive processes directly linked to colonisation and capitalism: feral animals, exotic weeds, land clearing and habitat loss, changed fire regimes, pathogens, pollution, and salinity. These threats are clearly documented in regular State of the Australian Environment reports. A significant Indigenous Caring for Country environmental movement has emerged organically, seeking to address these threats and so maintain or enhance the biodiversity values of Indigenous lands; several thousand Aboriginal and Torres Strait Islander people work for wages or for welfare in Aboriginal ranger groups (Altman and Kerins 2012). This is an emerging fundamental alternative to extractive capitalism that is of environmental benefit to Australia at large.

I have undertaken research in remote Australia for over 40 years. In the last two decades I have developed a grounded model termed 'the hybrid economy' that looks to explain the nature of existing Indigenous economies (Altman 2010; Curchin 2019). This theorisation indicates that Indigenous landowners are currently looking to creatively combine elements of the customary (Indigenous), state (public) and market (private) sectors of their economies in pursuit of livelihoods that are diverse but fundamentally different from mainstream market capitalism.

The provision of environmental services is just one of myriad ways Indigenous people look to eke out a living, sometimes assisted by the settler state and sometimes hindered by its regulatory and other restrictions. Some illustrative examples from my research include: self-provisioning through the deployment of customary and local ecological knowledge to exercise native title rights to hunt endemic and exotic species as food for livelihood; locally controlled commodification of elements of the sacred geography to engage with global fine art and tourist art markets; engaging in cultural tourism ventures; and selling wild foods commercially. A recent innovation has been in the commodification of refigured savanna burning to reduce carbon emissions and earn crypto commodities called Australian Carbon Credit Units (ACCUs), some purchased by the Australian Government's Emissions Reduction Fund, some sold in the emerging carbon voluntary market. An innovator in this field is Arnhem Land Fire Abatement (NT) Limited (ALFA), a wholly owned Aboriginal company that collaborates with nine Aboriginal ranger groups across 80,000 sq. kms of Arnhem Land. ALFA has earned 3 million ACCUs in the last five years, returning $30 million to its members; its activity more than offsets the entire greenhouse gas emissions by the region's population of over 20,000 people.

Better options are also emerging for forms of extraction from Indigenous-owned lands that will yield far less environmentally destructive financial benefits than mining. One possibility for agreement making and benefit sharing is the generation of zero emissions renewable energy: Indigenous titled lands are exposed to some of the highest levels of solar irradiation in the world. Some corporations are quickly recognising this and negotiating agreements for multi-billion-dollar developments on Indigenous land like the massive Sun Cable project. Decarbonisation, emission avoidance, and carbon sequestration will all require access to Indigenous land, knowledge, and labour.

The hybrid economy represents a postcolonial prospect that directly challenges the settler colonial project to re-possess and exploit territories suitable for accumulation by dispossession (Harvey 2010). It is a model that represents the bundling together of a suite of activities diversely and productively. Where it flourishes, it generates more equitable outcome to the situations favoured by the settler state—where some Indigenous people have formal employment and the majority are unemployed and vulnerable to the neoliberal governmentality—and to draconian regimes of mutual obligation conditionality that sees more than 50 per cent of remote Indigenous households struggling below the poverty line despite their extensive land holdings.

It is important to note that market-based and extractive forms of capitalism might form a variable proportion of the hybrid economy form of provisioning, depending on the choices made by Indigenous landowners and communities. However, in the post-capitalist futures I envisage, capitalism will not be the singular privileged mode of production as currently proposed by powerful vested interests; nor will its dominant purpose be mineral extraction. Indeed, engagements with capitalism and the state as demonstrated in the ALFA example show how financial returns from the partial commodification of savanna burning can be repurposed to finance ranger groups to 'care for country' in accord with Indigenous landowner aspirations informed by custom.

'At times of crisis the irrationality of capitalism becomes plain for all to see,' notes David Harvey (2010). At present, it seems not plain enough for those in power; or maybe too plain and in need of destructive bolstering? In Canada, Dene academic and activist Glen Coulthard (2013) argues persuasively that for Indigenous nations to survive, capitalism must die, and more constructively he suggests that for capitalism to die, Indigenous peoples must actively participate in alternatives to it. In Australia there are too few Indigenous proposals to undermine the state and corporate powers that jointly and unilaterally structure the possibilities and choices available to Indigenous people. The dominant voices of some Indigenous spokespeople, like Noel Pearson, have given moral authority to the 'real' economy or capitalism as the only future; this represents an acquiescence to the seductive invitation to participate in what Steven Schnoor (2017) has termed 'accumulation by self-dispossession'.

Proposals by Indigenous public intellectuals like Michael Mansell (2016) for the creation of an Indigenous sovereign state and different post-capitalist futures are ignored in public and policy debates. Such radical proposals that will require effective political representation and new jurisdictions fundamentally challenge current neoliberal arrangements that perpetuate Indigenous marginality. The hegemonic settler state continually colludes with major corporations to dilute legally-won native title rights and interests so as to accelerate extraction; and to depopulate homelands, the discrete Indigenous communities in Fig. 12.1, those populated dots in the landscape whose residents might have alternate views of what constitutes 'development'.

As I write this during the COVID-19 pandemic, Prime Minister Scott Morrison is looking to 'snap back' the economy and society to a pre-pandemic ex ante form of rampant capitalism. This imaginary is reminiscent of the old 'develop the north' way of thinking as articulated by Alfred Deakin that has always served Indigenous Australians badly. Some of the transformations that Indigenous people have managed in recent decades as they repossessed their ancestral lands have been impressive. But any transformation to post-capitalist futures for Indigenous people with land title faces two critical challenges: where is the pathway, and how might such a transition be financed. Part of the answer to the first challenge must be political activism for forms of resurgence and decolonisation Indigenous people desire. Part of the answer to the second needs to be from a combination of economic justice reparations to compensate peoples and country for damages done; plus, equitable payments for national and global benefits delivered. Imagining a move to such a post-capitalist future, a 'snapping forward' rather than a 'snapping back', is more than mere idealistic utopianism in the uncertain present; it is essential for Indigenous survival as well as for the nation.

References

Altman, Jon. 2010. What Future for Remote Indigenous Australia: Economic Hybridity and the Neoliberal Turn. In *Culture Crisis: Anthropology and Politics in Aboriginal Australia*, ed. Jon Altman and Melinda Hinkson. Sydney: UNSW Press.

Altman, Jon, and Sean Kerins. 2012. *People on Country, Vibrant Landscapes, Indigenous Futures*. Sydney: The Federation Press.

Altman, Jon, and Francis Markham. 2015. Burgeoning Indigenous Land Ownership: Diverse Values and Strategic Potentialities. In *Native Title from Mabo to Akiba: A Vehicle for Change and Empowerment?* ed. Sean Brennan, Megan Davis, Brendan Edgeworth, and Leon Terrell. Sydney: Federation Press.

Australian Government. 2015. *Our North, Our Future: White Paper on Developing Northern Australia*. Accessed June 3, 2020. https://www.industry.gov.au/sites/default/files/June%202018/document/pdf/nawp-fullreport.pdf?acsf_files_redirect.

Coulthard, Glen. 2013. For Our Nations To Live, Capitalism Must Die. In *Unsettling America: Decolonization in Theory and Practice*. Accessed June 4, 2020. https://unsettlingamerica.wordpress.com/2013/11/05/for-our-nations-to-live-capitalism-must-die/.

Curchin, Katherine. 2019. Economic Hybridity in Remote Indigenous Australia as Development Alterity. In *Postdevelopment in Practice: Alternatives, Economies, Ontologies*, ed. Elise Klein and Carlos Morreo. London: Routledge.

Harvey, David. 2010. *The Enigma of Capital and the Crisis of Capitalism*. New York: Oxford University Press.

Mansell, Michael. 2016. *Treaty and Statehood: Aboriginal Self Determination*. Sydney: The Federation Press.

Schnoor, Steven. 2017. A Vulture is Not a Dove: The Politics of Indigeneity and Resistance to Canadian Extractivism in the Americas. *Media Tropes* VII (1): 97–165.

Wolfe, Patrick. 2006. Settler Colonialism and the Elimination of the Native. *Journal of Genocide Research* 8 (4): 387–409.

14

Environmental Justice Movements as Mediums of Post-Capitalist Futures: Perspectives from India

Brototi Roy

Environmental defenders are people and collectives resisting projects and activities which damage the environment and result in the disproportionate distribution of harms to marginalised communities in the name of capitalist growth and 'development' (Scheidel et al. 2020). They spearhead and mobilise environmental justice movements, often at great personal physical and emotional costs, to protect and preserve nature and culture, across extractive commodity frontiers.

The literature on environmental justice movements, as we know it today, was conceptualised around environmental racism in the USA (Bullard 1993). Laura Pulido (2017) argues that environmental racism stems from pre-existing racial violence which is a fundamental element of contemporary capitalism. She calls such environmental justice movements manifestations of *subaltern environmental struggles* (Pulido 1996). Joan Martinez-Alier (2003) calls them *environmentalism of the poor*.

B. Roy (✉)
Institute of Development Policy, University of Antwerp, Antwerp, Belgium
e-mail: brototi.roy@uantwerpen.be

It is not surprising that Indigenous and marginalised communities are at the forefront of many such environmental justice movements, since historically they have faced multiple levels of socio-ecological injustices. It is also not surprising to find that Indigenous environmental defenders across the globe face a disproportionate impact of violence and repressions while trying to defend land, water, culture, and heritage, and defending worldviews different from the capitalist logic of profit motives.

In this chapter, I will first provide evidence of who the Indigenous peoples of India are and how they are disproportionately affected by capitalist notions of development, along with a brief history of environmental justice movements in India. This will be followed by discussion of one such case of indigenous resistance against a bottling plant of Coca-Cola in the South Indian state of Kerala, and the post-capitalist visions it encompassed. I will conclude with insights from an Adivasi activist and poet on what is understood as 'real' development, and what visions are presented by Indigenous communities. These resistances and activists articulate post-capitalist futures by providing alternative visions of living and wellbeing.

Environmental Defenders as Agents for Post-Capitalist Futures

In recent years, many studies and reports have highlighted the invaluable efforts of environmental defenders and movements for global sustainability and just futures, including the United Nations Human Rights Council. My own collaborative research using the largest online database on environmental justice movements in the world, the Environmental Justice Atlas (www.ejatlas.org), highlights the importance of grassroots environmental justice activism and bottom-up resistances for a more just and sustainable world (Scheidel et al. 2020).

In India too, many projects of land grabbing, commercial plantations, mining and other extractive industries, all in the name of development, have resulted in large-scale displacement of the poor and marginalised communities. In the absence of official figures, grassroots organisations and intellectuals have estimated that more than 60 million people have been adversely affected, either due to displacement or to lost livelihoods, since India's independence in 1947 (Shrivastava and Kothari 2012).

This development-induced displacement disproportionately affects the Adivasis, the Indigenous population of India. Literally translated as the first or ancient dwellers, and officially classified as 'Scheduled Tribes', Adivasis in India comprise more than 700 different tribes. According to the 2011 census data, 8.6% of India's total population (more than 100 million people) identify as Adivasis. Depending on their geographical location, different sets of laws apply to them. The Adivasis of peninsular India are largely found in the states of Andhra Pradesh, Chhattisgarh, Gujarat, Jharkhand, Madhya Pradesh, Maharashtra, Odisha, Rajasthan, and West Bengal.

Estimates suggest more than 40% of the people affected or displaced in the name of development are Adivasis, mostly from peninsular India (Shrivastava and Kothari 2012). According to the Environmental Justice Atlas, more than half of the environmental justice movements in India (57%) involve Indigenous people mobilising. The main motivation behind these movements, and the post-capitalist visions they encompass, are captured by these lines:

> We will not leave our village,
> Nor our forests, Nor our mother earth,
> We will not give up our fight!
> They built dams, drowned villages and built factories,
> They cut down forests, dug out mines, built sanctuaries,
> Without water, land and forest, where do we go?
> Oh God of Development, do tell us, how to save our lives?
> –Gaon Chhodab Nahi, *We Will Not Leave Our Village*

These lines are the lyrics of the opening stanza of a protest song against the continued destruction of the environment and people in the name of capitalist growth and development in India. It was inspired by a song sung by Bhaghwan Maaji, an Adivasi leader fighting against bauxite mining in Kashipur, in the east Indian state of Odisha in the early 2000s. The song goes on to explain how the current destruction of nature and marginalised communities are being carried out due to the growth imperatives of capitalism—where the politicians and the private corporations are in collusion and only interested in profit margins. It describes how this results in the sacrifice of the health and wealth of the planet and its people in the name of economic growth. The lyrics poetically suggest that a sustainable and equitable future cannot be attained if we allow such crony capitalism to continue and calls for environmental defenders to unite to save the earth and the people from this destruction.

A Brief History of India's Environmental Justice Movements

Although the Chipko Movement, which started in March 1973, is often credited as the first environmental justice movement of India, the history of such resistances in the country can be traced back much further. Early grassroots resistances to British rule, such as the Santhal revolt of 1855, the Indigo Revolt of 1859–1863, and the protests in Gudem-Rampa in the 1920s, were due to alienation of land and expropriation of forests (Guha 2007). Birsa Munda, an Adivasi hero of the fight for freedom against colonialism in the late 1800s, in today's context could be considered a leader of environmental justice struggles. He fought to safeguard the forests and their resources, as well as indigenous autonomy over those forests and resources. Many Indigenous struggles today remember and invoke Birsa's bravery and persistence fighting against extraction and injustices.

Mahatma Gandhi's freedom movement too rang with concerns for the ecosystem. The base of the movement inhabited the seven hundred thousand villages of the nation, and advocated a model of self-sufficiency and opposition to industrialisation. In 1928, Gandhi said, 'The economic imperialism of a single tiny island kingdom [England] is today keeping the world in chains. If an entire nation of 300 million [India] took to similar economic exploitation, it would strip the world bare like locusts.'

Unfortunately, after independence in 1947, there was a heavy boost to large infrastructure for nation building, such as multi-purpose dam projects and intensive mining of iron ore, coal, and other natural resources. This focus on rapid industrialisation ushered in a wave of environmental justice movements in the country that fought for the preservation of water, forest, and land (*jal, jungle, jameen*). The patterns of these development projects are a continuation of colonial extraction and exploitation. In fact, scholars have explained the intricate links between colonialism and capitalism, and how both depend(ed) on large-scale extraction of natural resources and exploitation of marginalised communities (Dey 2010). The historical plight of the Adivasis is a key example in the Indian context.

The Environmental Justice Atlas is a tool for collaborative research on ecological distribution conflicts with a global perspective. It shows that India has the highest number of cases of environmental justice conflicts in the world. As of June 2020, out of more than 3200 cases globally, 334 were reported from India.

Out of these 334 cases, 151 are high-intensity cases, with mass mobilisations and widespread and often violent engagements, such as arrests and bodily harm to the environmental defenders, and 136 cases are medium-intensity ones with visible mobilisations such as street protests. In total, about 86% of the environmental justice conflicts in India have some form of visible mobilisation. Indigenous or traditional communities are involved as protestors in nearly 60% of all the cases from India.

Examining these 334 cases reveals a variety of post-capitalist motivations for resisting development projects from across the country. In the north-east, there is a movement for the rejection of the Etalin hydroelectric dam project because it would completely alter the rich biodiversity as well as the cultural heritage of the Idu-Mishmi Indigenous community in Dibang Valley in Arunachal Pradesh. The only logic for building a $3.3 million hydel project in a region of high seismic activity with 350 glacial lakes upstream, displacing Indigenous people and destroying a biodiverse rich forest is the capitalist logic of growth. The movement against this dam and for saving the Dibang Valley reiterates the argument that profits cannot be put before people and planet.

Similarly, in central India, environmental defenders are fighting against the creation of a metro car shed, the building of which involves felling thousands of trees in Mumbai's Aarey Forest, the last green lungs of the city as well as home of the Warli Indigenous community. Here too, the resistance is against the logic of profit motives, and for human and environmental wellbeing. Both these movements, along with many others in the country, reject the narrow capitalist notion of development.

Instead, there are articulations of different visions and alternatives to the inequitable and unsustainable model of development. One such alternative is *radical ecological democracy*, which can be understood as a socio-cultural, political, and economic arrangement in which all people and communities have the right and full opportunity to participate in decision-making, based on the twin fulcrums of ecological sustainability and human equity (Kothari 2014). In the next section, I look at a concrete example of one such mobilisation and its alternative visions.

The Plachimada Declaration as an Example of Post-Capitalist Resistance

The story of a protest of a little hamlet in the south of India against the corporate giant Coca-Cola shows the strength and perseverance of marginalised Indigenous communities, as well as a collaboration of different sectors of society to fight against destructive projects for economic growth.

In 2000, Hindustan Coca-Cola Beverages Private Ltd. (HCBLP), one of Coca-Cola's subsidiary companies, started operating a bottling plant in the hamlet of Plachimada, in Palakkad district in the South Indian state of Kerala. The company had received clearances to produce 561,000 litres of beverage per day and extract about 2 million litres of water daily. By the end of 2000, the villagers, mostly Indigenous population, started to get sick as the water had turned unsuitable for drinking and cooking. Agriculture had also started to be severely affected, which raised further concerns since this region is dependent on crop production as a source of livelihood. The chemical waste of the plant was also dumped on land without any treatment, further polluting the agricultural fields as well as the canals and wells, creating severe health hazards (Bijoy 2006).

After months of waiting for some action to be taken, on 22 April 2002 affected local people formed a network known as the Coca-Cola Virudha Janakeeya Samara Samithy (Anti Coca-Cola People's Struggle Committee), consisting of more than 1500 members, mostly Adivasis, with demands to immediately shut down the plant. The protesters were threatened with violence from police and private security, with frequent arrests, threats, and false cases. However, a group consisting mostly of Adivasi women continued their public protests in the form of blockades, marches, public rallies, and sit-ins and it slowly turned into a popular struggle, with the formation of a Plachimada Solidarity Committee consisting of 32 organisations from across the state, including a diverse set of actors (Bijoy 2006).

Mylamma, an Adivasi woman without any background of formal education, who understood how the plant was turning the water toxic due to her lived realities, started the movement against Coca-Cola in Plachimada. This was complemented by the Perumatty panchayat (local village council) filing a public interest litigation in the Kerala High Court against Coca-Cola as well as mounting resistance from national and international water activists. These resistances involved protests against Coca-Cola plants from other parts of the country, highlighting the degraded water quality as a result of misconduct through public rallies and media campaigns, as well as the lack of employment in the region, which was earlier promised to be a result of the bottling plant. In 2004, as a result of these protests and the mounting evidence of criminality, the Coca-Cola plant was shut down.

The movement also created synergies with other similar resistances, and by May 2004 a network called Coca Cola Pepsi Cola Quit India Campaign brought together groups fighting against water mining in Delhi. India has 87 other Coca-Cola and Pepsi plants where, similarly, water is being polluted and depleted.

The Plachimada Declaration shows the non-capitalist understanding and articulation of this environmental justice movement (Shiva 2005).

> ### *The Plachimada Declaration*
>
> Water is the basis of life; it is the gift of nature; it belongs to all living beings on earth.
>
> Water is not private property. It is a common resource for the sustenance of all.
>
> Water is the fundamental human right. It has to be conserved, protected, and managed. It is our fundamental obligation to prevent water scarcity and pollution and to preserve it for generations.
>
> Water is not a commodity. We should resist all criminal attempts to marketise, privatise, and corporatise water. Only through these means can we ensure the fundamental and inalienable right to water for people all over the world.
>
> The water policy should be formulated on the basis of this outlook.
>
> The right to conserve, use, and manage water is fully vested with the local community. This is the very basis of water democracy. Any attempt to reduce or deny this right is a crime.
>
> The production and marketing of the poisonous products of the Coca-Cola and Pepsi-Cola corporations lead to total destruction and pollution and also endanger the very existence of local communities.
>
> The resistance that has come up in Plachimada, Puducherry, and in various other parts of the world is the symbol of our valiant struggle against the devilish corporate gangs who pirate our water.
>
> We, who are in the battlefield in full solidarity with the Adivasis who have put up resistance against the tortures of the horrid commercial forces in Plachimada, exhort the people all over the world to boycott the products of Coca-Cola and Pepsi-Cola.
>
> Coca Cola- Pepsi Cola "quit India".

Such environmental justice movements are often criticised as being anti-development. The capitalist narrative that a bottling plant by Coca-Cola will usher in economic growth and prosperity has been frequently challenged and in multiple formats—from academic articles to documentaries. And yet, the status quo remains the same.

In such circumstances, the questions of development for whom and at what cost become very crucial. In the Indian context it becomes equally pertinent for a decolonial understanding of environmental justice movements to ask the people who have suffered the most from such capitalist projects, the Adivasis, about their understanding of development.

An Adivasi Understanding of a Post-Capitalist Utopia

In this section, I describe a short conversation with my friend Jacinta Kerketta on what a post-capitalist utopia would look like for her. Jacinta Kerketta is an Indigenous poet, journalist, and social activist hailing from the central Indian state of Jharkhand and belonging to the Oraon tribe. She has grown up witnessing and participating in the struggle of the vast Adivasi society to preserve their land, forests, rivers, languages, and heritage and culture, which she expresses in her poetry.

According to her, the very concept of 'development' used in today's justification for extractive projects by imposing on a marginal community is flawed. She says, 'The first fundamental thing to question is this very concept of how one individual or a group of individuals can claim to "develop" another individual or society. Development for me implies a life of dignity. And that necessarily implies respect and understanding of the indigenous way of life. You can't develop someone if you consider yourself superior to them, that only leads to oppression.'

She further says, 'The present model of development in India is an imposition; it is an imposition on the Adivasi way of life. The Adivasis are strongly connected with nature—our words, rituals, culture and traditions all revolve around nature. We don't consider ourselves superior, but rather just a part of nature. Hence, we don't want to live at the cost of harming other plants and animals. However, the current model of development is based on the premise of looting the natural resources, be it the forests or the minerals underneath it. In other words, the current model, for us, is destruction in the name of development. It feels very hollow and fake to me. How can you call something which destroys forests, rivers, hills and mountains for monetary gains as development? That will only lead to protests and conflicts, as you can see everywhere in the country right now.'

She adds, 'I see the current development model to be a way to fulfil the selfish needs of the ruling capitalist class. Imposing a completely different belief system—one of looting and plundering of nature—would never sit well with the Adivasis. However, my development utopia would involve a path where the inherent customs and traditions of the Adivasi life are not mocked or ridiculed, like they are currently being done. Rather, there is an attempt to understand more about Adivasi language, songs, festivals, rituals and dialogue with them. We want schools and hospitals and roads, but not at the cost of destroying our traditional ecological knowledge or preaching to us that our religion and language and customs and way of life are inferior in any way. My utopia is one of dialogue and debate to reach the real meaning of development.'

Such articulations of environmental defenders also invoke the need for autonomy and dignity of the Indigenous communities and ways of life, which are brimming with post-capitalist solutions. As activists, scholars, and scholar-activists, we have a responsibility to give space to these ideas and actions of Indigenous communities, not just in India but everywhere; to learn with and from the diverse multiple ways of moving away from the capitalist system. This calls for a decolonising research and activism agenda, without imposing ideas, identities, and knowledges onto others.

References

Bijoy, C.R. 2006. Kerala's Plachimada Struggle: A Narrative on Water and Governance Rights. *Economic and Political Weekly* 41 (41): 4332–4339.

Bullard, Robert Doyle. 1993. *Confronting Environmental Racism: Voices from the Grassroots*. Boston: South End Press.

Dey, Dipankar. 2010. Inclusive Growth and Sustainable Development in India: A Case of Internal Colonialism. Accessed May 25, 2020. https://doi.org/10.2139/ssrn.1648744.

Guha, Ramachandra. 2007. Adivasis, Naxalites and Indian Democracy. *Economic and Political Weekly* 11: 3305–3312.

Kothari, Ashish. 2014. Radical Ecological Democracy: A Path Forward for India and Beyond. *Development* 57 (1): 36–45.

Martinez-Alier, Joan. 2003. *The Environmentalism of the Poor: A Study of Ecological Conflicts and Valuation*. Cheltenham: Edward Elgar Publishing.

Pulido, Laura. 1996. *Environmentalism and Economic Justice: Two Chicano Struggles in the Southwest*. Tuscon: University of Arizona Press.

———. 2017. Geographies of Race and Ethnicity II: Environmental Racism, Racial Capitalism and State-sanctioned Violence. *Progress in Human Geography* 41(4): 524–533. Accessed May 25, 2020. https://doi.org/10.1177/0309132516646495.

Scheidel, Arnim, et al. 2020. Environmental Conflicts and Defenders: A Global Overview. *Global Environmental Change* 63, 102104. Accessed May 25, 2020. https://doi.org/10.1016/j.gloenvcha.2020.102104.

Shiva, Vandana. 2005. *Earth Democracy: Justice, Sustainability and Peace*. London: Zed Books.

Shrivastava, Aseem, and Ashish Kothari. 2012. *Churning the Earth: The Making of Global India*. New Delhi: Penguin.

15

Careful Thinking: Pensar Cuidando—Henvupen Yaconso

Camila Marambio, Hema'ny Molina, and Bárbara Saavedra

Introduction

Hema'ny Molina, Selk'nam activist and writer, Bárbara Saavedra, Chilean ecologist, and Camila Marambio, liminal mestiza curator, unite in a pluriversal chorus of praise and forewarning. Their textual assemblage is intended as a remedy of the wounds inflicted on them by careless thinking, colonialism, objectification, patriarchy, and most of all by the lack of economic diversity that capitalist hegemony imposes on them, which by extension erodes the biodiversity of the lands that they care for. Embedded in the history and stewardship of the most austral peatlands on the planet, the bogs of Karokynka/Tierra del Fuego in the Chilean Patagonia,

---

C. Marambio (✉)
Ensayos, Tierra del Fuego, Chile

H. Molina
Hach Sayé, Porvenir, Chile

B. Saavedra
WCS Chile, Santiago, Chile

Hema'ny, Bárbara, and Camila set out to repair the erosion of diversity by way of plural *conversations*. They conjure an ethics of *conservation* that assembles Indigenous, environmental, aesthetic, and *swampy* sensibilities. They think carefully and apply their conscious nature to the combination of their words. Saturated with vulnerability, tenderness, and conviction, they recognise that they need each other and depend on their relationship to thrive. The economy of their care derives from the coalitional love that they practice.

> We three women feel for peat.
> Our feelings border on the fractured sense of who *we* are.

In Bárbara's tongue—ecology—a peatbog is a type of wetland. A wetland is an ecosystem dominated by water. Peat is accumulated decaying vegetal matter in a state of semi-decomposition. This phenomenon is due to a combination of constant water saturation, low levels of oxygen, and high levels of acidity that inhibit the survival of decomposing organisms. As the director of the Wildlife Conservation Society (WCS)-Chile, a global NGO that manages a 300,000-hectare wildlife preservation area on Karokynka/Tierra del Fuego, Bárbara works to conserve the 27 per cent of Karukinka Natural Park that is peatland. Her recent efforts concentrate on the urgent need to protect it from mining, agriculture, and invasive species.

In Hema'ny's tongue—Selk'nam chan—peatbogs are called hol-hol. Hema'ny is the president of the Selk'nam Corporation Chile. She lives in exile, 3400 kilometres north of her ancestral lands, in Santiago, the capital of Chile. She holds a national passport stating that she is a Chilean citizen and aches to be recognised by Chile as a citizen of the Indigenous nation of Karokynka/Tierra del Fuego. In collaboration with Bárbara, she has been training in peatbog conservation science. The accumulation of decaying peat moss, or *Sphagnum*, a genus of the approximately 380 non-vascular plants or mosses that grow on the bog, is a process that occurs over thousands of years. In this slow, invisible dance between life and death, dead *Sphagnum* become a carbon sink, maintaining biodiversity and also storing large quantities of freshwater. The anerobic atmosphere of hol-hol conserves whatever becomes trapped in its semi-decomposing body. Peatbogs are thus like living museums that can be considered great protectors of archaeological patrimony that we must take nothing from. They speak to us of the past and protect the ecosystem for the future. In addition to this, they are habitats for innumerable species of flora and fauna.

In Camila's tongue—curation—peatbogs are living metaphors of Earth time. Waterlogged, nutrient-rich, underrecognised, mushy, *las turberas* (peatbogs in Spanish) are bodies of water deserving of care and attention for no other reason than that they are of this world. Camila is the founder of Ensayos, a nomadic research programme that considers Karokynka/Tierra del Fuego the centre of the world. For a decade, she has been bringing together artists, scientists, and other local stakeholders to exercise emergent forms of place-based eco-cultural ethics. Camila introduced Bárbara to Hema'ny in 2019 and soon after the three of them started to explore how to co-care for the peatbogs of Patagonia.

Since their journey began not long ago, they want to acknowledge that what you are about to read is an *ensayo*, a creative experiment dedicated to peatbog conservation that, in this case, takes shape as an informal essay. The writing of which is characterised by personal experiences, individual inclinations, professional permutations, and joint revelations. In this *ensayo* Hema'ny, Bárbara, and Camila are co-learning bog-speak.

Acknowledgments

By way of respect, let us begin by telling you a little bit about Selk'nam country. Karokynka was inhabited over 8000 years ago by Selk'nam people, also known as Ona. Selk'nam history has been officially narrated by countless historians, anthropologists, and researchers; none of them Selk'nam. All of the academics have coincided on one thing: that Selk'nam people are extinct. Hema'ny takes a deep breath, she is alive.

Until early 2020, the Chilean state also presumed Selk'nam people to be extinct. As Hema'ny will point out, this is due, in part, to state-endorsed extermination policies which in 1883 gave way to the last stage of colonisation of Karokynka. The granting of Selk'nam lands to the

Wehrhahn Company, a sheep ranching venture, triggered an indirect Chilean state-promoted genocide. Genocide that lasts until today.

During the early days of colonisation, Selk'nam people were massacred, murdered, commercialised, and their children given away through illegal adoption. This is how Selk'nam bodies disappeared from plain sight. Only the attempts made by Salesian missions, namely San Rafael on Isla Dawson (Chile) and La Candelaria in Rio Grande (Argentina), tried to put an end to the killing and abuse. The results of their efforts, however, weren't successful. The Indigenous population was decimated at the missions due to confinement and illnesses.

A small group survived; they are the Rafaela Ishton Selk'nam Indigenous community of Argentina. In Chile, the surviving Indigenous inhabitants of Karokynka were exiled and violently made to assimilate. Children were given away or sold. Teenagers were enrolled in the military or made to work on saltpeter mines in the north of the country. Some were not removed from the island; however, they were made to work as unpaid labour on the livestock ranches themselves. In dire conditions, they had to make do. It was assumed by ranchers that if they didn't dress in Selk'nam customary clothes and didn't speak Selk'nam chan, they would stop being Selk'nam. This is an untruth.

Most of the ranching in Tierra del Fuego continues to ruin the health of the soil of the Selk'nam Nation. The pounding feet of the introduced bovines releases into the atmosphere more carbon than Gaia can seemingly handle, while displacing native icons like guanacos.

The final official erasure of the Karokynka peoples from existence occurred through the concealment of the identity of the children born to Selk'nam mothers raped by ranchers. These children were generally classified as mestizos. Giving way to the academically supported argumentation that 'pure' Indigenous peoples no longer existed.

The violent history of Karokynka's late colonisation was motivated by modernist ideologies of progress, economic productivity, and a political system that believes that trade and industry should be controlled by private owners for profit. The repercussions of this early capitalist mentality grew stronger as individuals profited not only from the land they stole from Indigenous peoples but, later, also from the tourist industry that thrived due to the lure of the myth of extinction promoted by academics.

15 Careful Thinking: Pensar Cuidando—Henvupen Yaconso

For the past 10 years, however, there has been a shift in consciousness.

As president of the Selk'nam Corporation Chile, Hema'ny spearheads the efforts of her people to be recognised as a living Indigenous community. Hema'ny thanks her ancestors for surviving, she still feels the pain of their enforced silencing, she admires their resilience, and she grieves their anonymity. She acknowledges that it is because of their silent grace that she can turn towards the conservation of her culture.

The Selk'nam Corporation's increasingly visible campaign to be legally recognised as a living community also owes its strength to the global Indigenous struggle. Around the world Indigenous communities speak up, lobby, and legislate for sovereignty of their native lands. In Chile this struggle has been compromised by the belief that mestizo people lose their ancestral rights to land, culture, and spirituality. A Selk'nam woman with green eyes is not entitled to be Selk'nam.

To obtain legal recognition for her people, and to strengthen Selk'nam cultural renaissance, appreciation, and identity within the community, is a colossal task that Hema'ny feels can only be achieved relationally. Selk'nam consanguineous kinship is strong; however, it is not the only kinship that binds voices in the joint struggle against the capitalist erasure of livelihoods. The process of deflecting the ignorance that exists around Selk'nam culture brings into being other alliances. Such as this one in the name of hol-hol.

Hema'ny learned of the urgency of conserving the peatbogs of Karokynka by way of Bárbara. Bárbara learned of Hema'ny by way of her work with Camila. Camila learned of Hema'ny by way of the peatbogs that Bárbara and she so often lie on to contemplate the future in the sky. Yes, this chain of interconnected knowing is animated by the practice of learning to listen to the more-than-human; an Ensayos experiment that began on the bogs of Karokynka during the early years of fieldwork for Ensayo #2: A Beaver Affair. During that time, Camila, along with the artist Christy Gast and Bárbara, amongst others, spent weeks at a time lying on the semi-decomposing bogs of Karukinka Natural Park attuning to the invasive beavers. The silence afforded by beavers gave Camila the opportunity to hear another voice. Carried by the wind, the ceremonial songs of Selk'nam peoples of the past broke open Camila's heart and she knew, right then and there, that what she had been taught about extinction was a fallacy. But to know something with the heart is different to knowing the facts about something, so Camila spent years tearing away at the problem of the misconstruction of Selk'nam extinction. She finally arrived at being able to see what was there (all along): Selk'nam people and culture, semi-decomposed, striving to exist. She allied herself to Hema'ny and thus began what is now taking shape in this essay.

The wordsmithing that ensues is a performative, speculative, science-based, Indigenously minded, aesthetic activity of *poderío* (power-with). A co-constitutive act of co-caring for the peatbogs of Karokynka/Tierra del Fuego and for each other. The feeling/thinking/seeing that went into writing each portion of the triadic essay is an incantation for and with the peatbogs of Karokynka/ Tierra del Fuego. By being deliberately boggy, no one can be stepped on alone.

Turba Tol/Heart of Peat, by Hemany

In the past, my elders, my ancestors lived in communion with all of that environment, which today is said to be in a state of extreme vulnerability. They were part of the landscape, and that's how they understood it. This is why they never took from nature if there was no real need for it; they didn't hoard things or keep things for the future, because Mother Earth always provided what was necessary for life, at the time and place in which it was required.

Yet with colonisation, the multiple interconnected values of our peatbogs were not recognised and worse still, their commercial value was privileged above everything else. This meant that peatbogs were exploited by humans, leading to serious damage. Peat is extracted for water purification systems and sold as a substrate in replacement of real soil, it is now being franchised for mining and water extraction activities.

The relationship we have with our ancestral territory is growing day by day. We were estranged from Karokynka, but as the people who currently inhabit our territory get to know us and respect our stories, they seek us out and we gain sovereignty. The belief that mestizo people lose their ancestral rights of custodianship of land and of cultural expression is changing, but the convenience of having an extinct culture to fuel a tourist industry is still our major problem. What's more, this interest in commercialising our culture is currently spreading all over the country. This is how the indiscriminate use of icons, language, and other cultural aspects is unscrupulously encouraged, in large part posing as a homage that incidentally leaves a profit for those who had and still have these commercial initiatives.

Some conventions and treaties have been signed to help defend some aspects of Indigenous peoples' sovereignty, such as ILO Convention 169 (2007) and the United Nations Declaration on the Rights of Indigenous Peoples. However, not much can be done in reality, since the interests of large transnational companies and private investors end up being prioritised, helping them to secure the territories that concentrate the most resources. Chile's Indigenous peoples, even those recognised and integrated under law (which we Selk'nam are not yet), have no authority over the regulations of use of their territories, culture, ancestral medicine, traditional clothing, and ancestral cultural expressions. Patagonian peatbogs have become an attractive new source of venture capital for different kinds of companies and uses.

Currently, we Selk'nam people do not live on our territory. Having been exiled during the colonisation of Tierra del Fuego, we can, however, combat the situation by strengthening or bonding from afar and in alliance with those who live there. One of the most important aspects of self-identification is to live spirituality as part of our lives and not as a myth or a legend that is narrated in books. Today, we are making arduous efforts to teach people to respect our spirituality as a living and everyday aspect of the way of our people.

This spiritual work has led me to see the peatbogs as the future. My dream is to share their value as a way of detoxifying the planet. They are a point of union in the hopeful path of human subsistence. I feel that understanding peatbogs, defending them, and helping them to keep growing is my responsibility as a human being, and as a Selk'nam woman.

Decolonising is Recognising, Valuing, Restoring, and Promoting the World's Biodiversity, by Bárbara Saavedra

Though under-recognised, the loss of biodiversity constitutes the largest global problem that humanity faces today, even more so than global warming. Unlike the CO_2 molecule—the greatest contributor to the increase in our planet's temperature is a molecule that is the same in every corner of the universe—biodiversity is unique to each place. This is the result of ecological-evolutionary processes that are complex, permanent, and often unrepeatable. This living web is specific and different in every territory on the planet and is especially rich in places that are farther away and isolated, like Tierra del Fuego. And above all in wetland ecosystems such as peatbogs. Conservation practice is a nonlinear construction. Like biodiversity it is a complex hypervolume that results from the strategies and actions that can or need to be implemented to change the trajectory of a conservation target, such as a peatbog, or some of their threats. Like biodiversity, conservation is context dependent and results from careful and well-informed planning, activated in the actual milieu of local/global realities—subject to funding, policies, capacities, interests, and many other factors—that exist in the permanent moment of action.

Though America is the world's largest reservoir of biodiversity, its nature has suffered the harsh effects of colonisation from very early on. The well-known massive-scale sheep farming in Patagonia, including Tierra del Fuego, brought along with it, amongst other things, the degradation of grassland ecosystems, one of the most degraded ecosystems in Chile, as well as the brutal impact on Selk'nam people and culture. Another more recent example is the production of flowers to adorn European balconies, which use peat and moss from the peatbogs of Patagonia.

Paradoxically, the loss of biodiversity can only be noticed once it has disappeared. Equally paradoxical is the fact that the global recovery of biodiversity requires efforts that are hyperlocal, because it is at that scale that life exists and is woven. Thus, one key for decolonisation is to bring

15 Careful Thinking: Pensar Cuidando—Henvupen Yaconso

back the American continent's *naturecultures*,[1] and to re-establish the relationships that are specific to its life, both human and non-human. This requires, first off, the recognition and appreciation of the biodiversity that is original to these latitudes, followed by the activation of processes that allow for its restoration and definitive return. It is around this process that the deep and intrinsic value of American diversity will be revealed, which in turn should elicit the commitment of not only the current inhabitants of this continent, but especially of the 'civilised' world, which must cease to satisfy its consumption needs through the degradation of our continent, our nature, and our people.

One of these actions was the establishment of the Karukinka Natural Park in 2004, the largest protected area on the main island of Tierra de Fuego, which has been managed by WCS, with me as the leader of that conservation project for 16 years. Karukinka Natural Park holds the largest peatlands of the province, threatened directly by mining, beaver invasion, and non-directly by lack of valuation. After careful planning, working at different scales and levels, we decided to focus our efforts on three pivotal points: promoting peatland value and conservation at the local and national level; protecting Tierra del Fuego's peatlands from direct threats; and integrating our conservation efforts at the Patagonian level.

In a still active conservation process, we have developed research and environmental education on peatlands for years, both for local and national stakeholders. With careful design and above all persistent presence, we have been able to raise awareness about Patagonian peatlands, their value as critical ecosystems for water and carbon balance, channeling interest and support. Because of this, we managed to get the protection of the Ministry of Mining, which prohibited mining activities in Karukinka Natural Park in 2014. As a result of this, the near 80,000 ha of peatlands that exist in southern Tierra del Fuego are now protected and devoted to research. In alliance with several stakeholders, both at the hyperlocal and national level, we are now leading the implementation of

---

[1] *natureculture* was coined by Donna J. Haraway in 2003 (Haraway, 2003) and synthesises nature and culture, recognising their inseparability in ecological relationships that are both biophysically and socially formed.

a large experiment, evaluating alternatives for beaver removal and peatland restoration. At a national level, we promoted and supported the inclusion of peatlands in the Nationally Determined Contributions—Chile's commitment to the global climate agreement—which we believe represents a nature-based pillar to guide Chile's carbon neutrality transformation by 2050. Being the stewards of the majority of Tierra del Fuego peatlands, which are the southernmost peatlands that exist in America and in the world, we expect to focus our efforts on the construction of a Patagonian Peatland Center, which can serve as a lighthouse of knowledge and integration—science and art, local and global, Selk'nam and mestizos, conservation and sustainable production—and guide us through the complex, uncertain, and urgent waters of a biodiversity conservation practice.

Where Is the Boat Going?, by Camila Marambio

In her book *Matters of Care*, María Puig de la Bellacasa (2017) advises that if we want to care for and repair the world in which we live, first, we have to learn to know it in different ways. She defends the idea that to leave behind fragmented and split reality, forged by modern epistemologies, we have to think the ethics of care from the point of view of a complex, open-I, that implies new alliances between humans and non-humans, alive and dead.

In the spirit of Puig de la Bellacasa's 'open-I', in Ensayos we perform children's songs as a way to amusingly educate ourselves (and others) about the possibilities of these 'unlikely' alliances. Some of these songs can be listened to via the Ensayos' website, under Listening Series (https://ensayostierradelfuego.net/category/programs/listening-series/). For the episode of Listening Series dedicated to peatbogs, the artist Christy Gast and I re-wrote the lyrics of *Onde va la Lancha?*, a folk song from the archipelago of Chiloe, a boggy wetland that lies north of Karokynka and north of Patagonia. In our version of the song, we respond to the question posed in the title *Where is the Boat Going?* with the refrain *La Turbera!* (peatbog in Spanish).

15   Careful Thinking: Pensar Cuidando—Henvupen Yaconso

Below are the lyrics for you, the reader, to join Hema'ny, Bárbara, and I in the act of harmonising our diversity and proclaiming the future as boggy. Since I have deliberately not translated the song into English, I've devised a score to guide you in the process of wading through a different language: First, read the song out loud. Pronounce the words in whichever way you can. Enjoy the way your tongue twists, notice the difficulties that arise, and delight in what you *can't* understand. Once you've read and heard the whole song in your own voice, you can go back and make sense of the bits you did grasp. Notice the coincidences between languages and write out what you think/feel the song says, fill in the gaps with your own knowledge of peatbogs. If you wish you can search for the translation of words or phrases whose meaning escapes you. Lastly, listen to the song online and enjoy the sounds of a small clan of Chileans improvising the melody while learning about La Turbera!

¿'Onde va la Lancha?
Turbera, turbera, con amor la lancha se va.
La expedición está lista, el zarpe aquí está,
científicas todas contentas se van.
De pronto una niña se acerca al pasar,
pregunta en voz alta ¿La lancha 'onde va?
¿'Onde va la lancha?! La turbera.
Turbera, turbera, con amor la lancha se va.
¿Qué es la turba? grita la niña.
Es un humedal, contestan las científicas.
Contiene material vegetal descompuesto,
filtra el agua y capta carbono.
¿'Onde va la lancha?! La turbera.
Turbera, turbera, con amor la lancha se va.
Es un ser vivo de doce mil años que corre peligro de ser minado.
Nos habla del pasado, hay que protegerla.
Nutre el futuro de la biodiversidad.
¿'Onde va la lancha?! La turbera.

If you followed the score I proposed, you've just experienced some of the back and forth that Hema'ny, Bárbara, and I have had to do to *write* this article. Our boggy process, between languages, across media, space and time, over personal and political histories is a labour grounded in an ethics of carefully feeling/thinking/seeing each other together and apart.

Translation is commonly an act of conversion; but what of a translation process that wants to sustain diversity, achieve confluence, and leave room for the unknowable? Sisterly translation is what I call my effort to translate in such a way that what the other has said or written is respected, opened up, and semi-decomposed all at once. The work of fusing cares, cultures, and concerns is an act of coalitional love (Sandoval 2000).

Closing Remarks

The bond that carries Hema'ny, Bárbara, and Camila through the murky disparities of their assemblage grows strong thanks to the joint quest to see beyond the end, towards a different past, towards a lively future, towards a carefully considerate present, in diversity. A present founded on the practice of equally valuing each perspective, as one does each piece of a jigsaw puzzle, looking to find its fit with the cultures of conservation. This is achieved by continually undoing the very notion of value upheld by each of the authors. Hema'ny, Bárbara, and Camila are not invested in making sense of each other. They care for the others' wor(l)ds. By attempting to feel/think/see together they entrust their power to the other and reveal their vulnerabilities, creating *poderío*.

> We have not made sense.
> We have resisted extinction.
> We have become each other.
> We thrive in diversity.
> We are not alone.
>
> We endure in trust
> and conserve our differences
> by caring-together for the same thing
> from multiple perspectives.

15 Careful Thinking: Pensar Cuidando—Henvupen Yaconso

We breathe life together,
and do this to breathe life
into the bodies and wetlands
that sustain our very breathing.

We stand on coalitions and dream of more.
The Patagonian Peatland Conservation Centre,
where a story-map
as dense as the bog itself
brings together
Selk'nam Chan,
scientific observations,
conservation practices
and artistic interventions.

We give thanks for opportunities,
like this one,
that give us the ground to create
and expand
a collaboratory experience.

We offer to the readers our method,
not as an original finding,
but as a humble construction
that aims to bridge feeling,
thinking,
seeing,
care,
and conservation.

As beginners we honour our backgrounds,
remain in the learning,
we do not claim expertise or power-over.
Our power arises with-with-with each other.
We stay in the with-with-with,
as curious children who sing songs to the bog.

References

Haraway, Donna J. 2003. *The Companion Species Manifesto: Dogs, People, and Significant Otherness*. Chicago: Prickly Paradigm Press.

Puig de la Bellacasa, María. 2017. *Matters of Care: Speculative Ethics in More Than Human Worlds*. Minneapolis, MN: University of Minnesota Press.

Sandoval, Chela. 2000. *Methodology of the Oppressed*. Minneapolis, MN: University of Minnesota Press.

Index[1]

A

Accumulate/accumulation, 3, 4, 45, 70, 71, 93, 110, 111, 114, 115, 136, 148, 149, 166

Activism/activist, 13, 14, 18, 32, 34–38, 42, 44, 46–51, 55, 61, 69, 110, 149, 150, 154, 159, 161, 162, 165

Alternative, v, 3–6, 8, 9, 11–15, 17, 19, 26, 29, 32, 33, 39, 47, 54–60, 62, 66, 70, 79, 80, 84, 108, 112, 114, 115, 120, 124, 129, 131, 136, 141–150, 154, 158, 174

Australia, 17, 67, 134, 138, 141–143, 145–147, 149

Authoritarian/authoritarianism, 5, 13, 14, 28, 29, 56, 66, 68–71, 73, 125

B

Banking, 23, 58, 89, 103, 120
Bioregional, 61

C

Capital/capitalism/capitalist, v, 1–18, 25–27, 31–35, 39, 41, 42, 44–47, 51, 53–59, 61–63, 65–73, 77–82, 89–94, 99, 103, 108, 110–115, 118–120, 124, 125, 129–139, 142, 145–147, 149, 150, 153–158, 160–162, 165, 166, 168, 169, 171

Capitalist realism, 7–11, 14, 18, 59

Carbon, v, 2, 10, 16, 79, 81, 87, 101, 122, 142, 148, 166, 168, 173, 174

---

[1] Note: Page numbers followed by 'n' refer to notes.

Care, 2, 5–7, 18, 47, 49, 50, 57, 79, 81–83, 85, 88–94, 139, 149, 165–167, 174, 176
China, 4, 14, 65–73
Class, 3, 16, 19, 24, 32, 49, 71, 111, 113–115, 161
Climate/climate change, 10, 16, 24, 58, 71, 72, 107, 117–125, 130, 142, 145, 174
Colonial/colonialism/colonisation, 2, 3, 10, 132, 142, 148, 156, 157, 165
Commodity/commodification, 3, 44, 67, 71, 73, 81, 82, 101, 103, 134, 148, 149, 153, 160
Commoning, vi, 38
Commons, vi, 6, 7, 38, 39, 47, 50, 60–62, 68, 78, 87, 111, 112, 135, 139, 147, 160
Communism/communist, 5, 27, 34, 37
Community, v, 19, 31, 32, 37–39, 46, 50, 57, 61, 62, 84, 88, 114, 130–136, 138, 139, 142, 144, 149, 153, 154, 156–158, 160–162, 168, 169
Community economies, v, 6, 14, 41–51
Consumerism, 34, 136, 137
Consumption, 7, 17, 23, 37, 57, 59, 61–63, 77, 80, 81, 88, 90, 94, 99, 101, 119, 137–138, 173
Coronavirus, 2, 13, 16, 23, 25, 104, 130
Corporate/corporation, 4, 17, 49, 61, 66–70, 78, 79, 102, 103, 111, 114, 119, 120, 130, 132, 135–137, 139, 145, 146, 148, 149, 156, 158, 160, 169
COVID/COVID-19, 1–2, 16, 24, 54, 83, 98, 103, 104, 117–125, 150
Crisis/crises, 1, 2, 4, 6, 7, 9–11, 13, 14, 16, 24, 25, 34, 36, 55–56, 60–63, 80, 88–90, 93, 101–104, 107, 108, 117–125, 149

Debt, v, 16, 58, 101–103, 120, 121, 123, 136
Decolonization/decolonisation/decolonising, 18, 36, 37, 55, 150, 162, 172–174
Decouple/decoupling, 77, 78, 99
Degrowth, vi, 11, 14, 15, 26, 31, 33, 36, 53–63, 81, 97–104, 119, 136, 139
Democratic/democracy, vi, 4, 5, 17, 26–29, 32, 34–36, 38, 46, 112, 118, 136, 138, 158, 160
Development, 2, 17, 18, 29, 33, 38, 47, 49, 70, 71, 85, 94, 97, 112–114, 133, 138, 141–150, 153–155, 157, 158, 160–162
Distribute/distribution/distributive, 7, 14, 15, 37, 39, 48, 49, 54, 55, 59, 94, 110, 130, 153, 157
Diversity, v, vi, 7, 13, 14, 17, 32, 37, 42–48, 50, 51, 129, 130, 131n2, 165, 166, 173, 175, 176

Ecofeminist, 15, 34, 87–94
Ecological civilisation, 72
Ecosocialist/ecosocialism, v, 13, 15, 33–39, 57, 59
Enclosures, 111, 132
Energy, v, 15–17, 35, 36, 38, 53, 54, 57, 58, 78, 82, 88, 99–101, 104, 110, 122, 123, 135, 137–138, 148
Environment, 2, 48, 51, 70, 132, 135, 146, 153, 155, 170
Environmental justice movements, 18, 153–162
Exploit/exploitation, 3, 9, 16, 18, 67, 90, 91, 94, 109, 113, 115, 132, 135, 136, 148, 156, 157

Far right, 13, 27–28
Feminist, 5, 88–92
Finance/financial, 9, 12, 14, 16, 17, 24, 25, 45, 47, 48, 53, 56–58, 61, 87, 88, 102–104, 107, 118, 121, 124, 135, 136, 148, 149
Food, 26, 31, 32, 37, 38, 46, 67, 79, 81, 123, 124, 130, 131, 133, 133n3, 134, 139, 148
Fully automated luxury communism (FALC), 77, 79, 85
Future, v, vi, 2–7, 9, 12–19, 32, 33, 39, 45, 51, 53, 56, 58, 66, 71–73, 77, 97, 98, 108, 109, 111–113, 115, 118, 120, 121, 123, 124, 129–135, 137–139, 145, 149, 150, 153–162, 167, 169–171, 175, 176

Gender, 3, 15, 34, 82, 84, 89, 91–94
Gibson-Graham, J.K., 6, 14, 42, 45, 46, 48, 62
Global Financial Crisis (GFC), 10, 13, 25, 120, 121
Globalisation, 1, 10, 25, 27, 29, 129, 133, 138, 139, 142
Global North, 2, 11, 13, 24, 25
Global South, 2, 13, 24, 25, 27, 28
Governance/government, 8, 15–17, 23, 27, 31, 33–39, 58, 60, 65–72, 77, 78, 81, 83, 84, 87, 103, 108, 110–112, 121, 123, 132, 134, 135, 142, 143
Grassroots, v, 13, 14, 32, 34–36, 38, 39, 54, 60, 61, 110, 112, 139, 154, 156
Green growth, 14, 15, 54, 63, 79, 93–94
Green New Deal (GND), vi, 10, 15, 24, 26, 87–94, 121
Gross Domestic Product (GDP), 15, 54, 57, 70, 83, 98–104, 120
Growth, vi, 4, 6, 8–11, 14–16, 54, 55, 58, 59, 63, 66, 70, 71, 77, 79–81, 87, 93–94, 98, 101, 103, 104, 111, 119, 120, 136, 143, 153, 155–158, 160

Haraway, Donna, 5, 173n1
Harvey, David, 4, 5, 59, 66, 148, 149
Holmgren, David, 58, 61
Hybrid economy, vi, 147–149

I

Imperialism, 2, 3, 156
India, 2, 18, 28, 34, 72, 129, 134, 153–162
Indigenous, 5, 17, 18, 32, 36, 38, 44, 63, 118, 133n3, 139, 141–150, 154–158, 161, 162, 166, 168, 169, 171
Inequality/inequalities, 3, 24, 25, 28, 59, 80–82, 84, 119, 124, 142

J

Justice, vi, 14, 15, 31, 35, 46, 53, 54, 59, 62, 89, 92, 94, 111, 112, 114, 115, 138, 150, 153, 154, 156, 157

K

Klein, Naomi, 34

L

Labour, 5, 16, 19, 44, 48, 50, 66, 70, 80, 84, 88–92, 94, 99, 100, 109, 111, 113–115, 133–135, 146, 148, 168, 176
Land, 17, 18, 32, 38, 44, 46, 47, 59, 68, 69, 82, 132–135, 141–150, 154–158, 161, 165–169, 171
Local/localisation, vi, 4, 5, 7, 17, 18, 35, 36, 38, 39, 44, 47, 61, 66, 69, 81, 82, 85, 110, 129–139, 147, 159, 160, 167, 172–174

M

Macroeconomics, 14, 15, 54, 97–104
Market, v, 3, 7, 9, 11–13, 15, 23, 32–35, 37–39, 44, 45, 54, 59, 61, 62, 66, 67, 70–72, 78–84, 89, 90, 92, 103, 111–114, 130, 131, 134, 145, 147, 148
Marx, Karl, 3, 33, 35, 37, 117
Mason, Paul, 79
Modern Monetary Theory, 16, 103, 121

N

Neoliberalism, 13, 23–30, 79
Non-monetary, 35, 38, 61

P

Pandemic, vi, 1, 2, 5, 8, 9, 11, 13, 16, 24, 25, 27, 54, 108, 118, 121, 130, 142, 150
Paradigm, 8, 11–15, 26, 28, 33, 35, 54–56, 58, 59, 61, 62
Paris Agreement, 122
Patagonia, 167, 172, 174
Piketty, Thomas, 9
Pluriverse, v, 39
Policy/policies, vi, 14, 15, 18, 32, 49, 50, 56–60, 67, 69–71, 73, 77, 87, 88, 91, 93, 94, 97, 98, 104, 110, 112, 113, 119, 121, 132, 133, 143, 145, 149, 160, 167, 172
Political economy, 1, 3, 4, 14, 15, 34, 53–56, 59, 62, 63, 79, 87–94

Politics, vi, 3, 11, 12, 14, 16, 17, 30, 34, 37, 54, 56, 59, 63, 78, 115
Population, 2, 16, 57–59, 79, 84, 98, 101, 114, 124, 142–145, 148, 155, 158, 168
Populism/populist, 5, 28
Post-capitalism/post-capitalist, v, 1–19, 31–34, 37, 39, 41–51, 53–56, 59–63, 71, 77, 79, 80, 82–84, 91, 107–115, 130, 131, 135–137, 139, 141–150, 153–162
Postcolonial, 134, 148
Post-development, 6, 13, 31–39, 55
Post-growth, 13, 33, 57, 58
Power, 6, 29, 35, 46, 54, 59, 62, 65, 66, 69–72, 78, 79, 88, 91, 92, 100, 101, 104, 108, 109, 111–113, 115, 123, 131, 132, 138, 149, 176, 177
Private property, 3, 44, 160
Production, v, 6–8, 14, 18, 23, 24, 35–39, 49, 57, 61–63, 65–73, 77–82, 88, 89, 92, 94, 99, 100, 108, 110, 112, 114, 115, 117–119, 135, 137, 142, 149, 158, 160, 172, 174
Progress, 10, 18, 57, 99, 121, 133, 168
Property, 44, 48, 59, 143, 145

Recession, 119, 121, 122
Rifkin, Jeremy, 78, 79, 88, 89
Right-wing, 5, 27, 50, 138

Social, 1, 3–5, 8, 9, 14, 15, 17, 23, 24, 26, 28, 29, 33, 35, 44, 46, 48–50, 54–62, 66–69, 72, 78, 80–85, 90, 92–94, 104, 107, 108, 111, 113–115, 117–120, 122–124, 131, 133, 136, 137, 161
Socialism/socialist, 4, 5, 12–14, 24, 26, 32–35, 37, 38, 79
Social movements, 6, 12, 14, 29, 37, 54, 60, 63, 112, 133
Social reproduction, 15, 89–91, 93, 94
State, v, vi, 4, 5, 13, 16, 19, 26, 27, 34–37, 47, 56, 60, 61, 68, 70, 71, 81, 83, 97, 103, 104, 107, 110, 115, 117–125, 132, 145–149, 154, 155, 158, 159, 161, 166, 167, 170
Streeck, Wolfgang, 4, 5, 8, 11, 120
Sufficiency, vi, 14, 32, 38, 53–63, 133
Sustainable/sustainability, v, 5, 9, 15, 33–35, 46, 48, 51, 53, 54, 57, 59, 60, 62, 72, 78, 81, 82, 85, 88, 91, 97, 121, 133, 142, 154, 156, 158, 174

Technology/technological, v, vi, 9, 15, 19, 34, 37, 54, 62, 77–85, 87, 88, 94, 107–109, 111–115, 135, 138

Transformation, v, vi, 16, 24, 26, 35, 36, 39, 46, 58, 59, 61, 65, 88, 112, 150, 174

Transition, 10, 13, 15, 16, 32, 53–60, 62, 63, 79, 80, 84, 85, 91, 107, 114, 119, 122, 123, 135, 150

Universal Basic Income (UBI), vi, 15, 24, 59, 80, 83, 84, 103

Universal Basic Services (UBS), vi, 15, 57, 59, 77–85

Urban, 14, 42, 45, 47, 49, 50, 66, 69, 82, 133, 145

Utopia/utopian/utopianism, 7, 15, 37, 66, 77–85, 107–115, 150, 161–162

Voluntary simplicity, 63

Wealth, 2, 46, 54, 59, 61, 62, 79, 82, 113, 118, 142, 156

Welfare state, 16, 27, 80, 119, 123, 124

Work/worker/working, vi, 2, 4–8, 12–14, 28, 32–34, 36, 38, 42, 44–47, 57, 61–63, 66, 67, 70, 78, 80, 83–85, 89–94, 98, 99, 101, 108–114, 129, 130, 133, 133n3, 134, 146, 147, 166, 168, 169, 171, 173, 176

Zero marginal cost, 15, 78, 79

GPSR Compliance

The European Union's (EU) General Product Safety Regulation (GPSR) is a set of rules that requires consumer products to be safe and our obligations to ensure this.

If you have any concerns about our products, you can contact us on

ProductSafety@springernature.com

In case Publisher is established outside the EU, the EU authorized representative is:

Springer Nature Customer Service Center GmbH
Europaplatz 3
69115 Heidelberg, Germany

www.ingramcontent.com/pod-product-compliance
Ingram Content Group UK Ltd.
Pitfield, Milton Keynes, MK11 3LW, UK
UKHW022154230426

12049UKWH00004BA/97